Penguin Education

**Penguin Education Specials**
*General Editor* Willem van der Eyken

Education for Democracy
Second Edition

Edited by David Rubinstein and Colin Stoneman

# Education for Democracy
## Second Edition

# Edited by David Rubinstein
# and Colin Stoneman

Penguin Books

Penguin Books Ltd, Harmondsworth,
Middlesex, England
Penguin Books Inc, 7110 Ambassador Road,
Baltimore, Md 21207, USA
Penguin Books Australia Ltd,
Ringwood, Victoria, Australia

First published 1970
Reprinted 1970
Second edition 1972
Copyright © David Rubinstein, Colin Stoneman
and contributors, 1970, 1972

Made and printed in Great Britain by
C. Nicholls & Company Ltd
Set in Monotype Plantin

# Contents

Part Five **Tertiary**

# Introduction

In no field has the division of the British people into social classes been more clearly demonstrated than in education. Throughout history the middle and upper classes, through their control of the economic, legislative and administrative apparatus, have given to the working classes as little and as poor an education as possible. When universal elementary education was finally introduced a century ago it was redolent with class assumptions. The dominant late-Victorian view was expressed by Lord George Hamilton, a former education minister, who declared that 'what was wanted was to give to the children of the working man a sound, a compact, and a thorough education in those subjects which children during the limited time they were at school could master' (*The Times*, 25 November 1891).

A similar attitude has been expressed on every occasion that attempts have been made to raise the school-leaving age, to improve access to secondary education for working-class children, or to open higher education to greater numbers. In 1935, for example, when the London County Council made its first tentative moves towards comprehensive secondary schools, its Education Officer, E. M. Rich, commented:

The great majority of London's children are destined to pursue occupations which will make little demand upon specialized gifts. . . . It is . . . important that those of less capacity should become aware of their own limitations, both as a spur to effort, and as an understanding of the conditions in which they are likely to enter adult life and the part they are likely to play in the life of the country (Quoted in Stuart Maclure, *One Hundred Years of London Education, 1870–1970*, 1970).

It was only after the social changes brought about by the Second World War that significant inroads were made into the pattern of subservience of education to the interests of a class society. Although there has been little change in the disparity of wealth, income and power since 1945, life styles have become more similar, not least due to the development of a new 'youth culture'. Surface inequalities have to some extent been ironed out, expectations have risen, and the effect has been felt on the educational system. More and more people are refusing to accept a system in which their children's lives are determined by selection at the age of eleven, or even earlier, by streaming in primary schools. Secondary education has become increasingly comprehensive in character and entrance to higher education has become possible for more people. At all levels, but particularly in the primary schools, more open methods have been introduced, concerned with stimulating and maintaining interest, educating *people* rather than training cogs for various parts of the industrial machine.

Progress since the war has been significant, but far from revolutionary. Even where the need for change has become generally recognized, the actual pace of change has remained slow.* Against the historical background of English society and English education, it is not surprising that there was a marked reaction from educational and political conservatives, coming to a head with the publication in 1969–70 of the three notorious Black Papers. These works, studded with a cluster of well-known names and sensational allegations, were a long series of protests against the development of progressive ideas and methods in all aspects of education. The Black writers, knowingly or not, put themselves squarely into the camp of those who had argued for so many decades that it was mistaken and dangerous to educate more than a handful of working-class children 'above their station'. But their unsubstantiated assertions were given

*For example, not only traditionalists but also Labour ministers have argued that far more British students are of working-class origin than in other Western European countries (Cox and Dyson (eds.), *Black Paper Two*, p. 49). 'It is a belief that has little if any foundation in fact', the Education Correspondent of *The Times* observed recently. A new study has shown that since 1947 Britain has fallen behind a number of other countries in offering opportunities in higher education to the working class (*The Times*, 6 October 1971). Here as in other fields, however, sober facts seem unlikely to stop extravagant claims of revolutionary change in educational opportunity.

wide publicity, and the first two Black Papers were followed by the election of a Conservative Government whose education policies, from the stopping of school milk to the protection of grammar and public schools, have moved towards the Black pattern.

The traditionalist position suggests that only by a system of elitist education can high standards be maintained. But the suspicion must arise that it is the elite rather than the standards which is the primary concern. 'When everybody is an M.A., nobody is', said the advance publicity for Black Paper Two, quoting the *Yorkshire Post* in support of the first Black Paper. This comes close to claiming that knowledge and research, even education itself, are of value only in so far as they control entry to the elite. It is such attitudes as these which foster the continuance of gross disparities in our education system, ensuring, for example, that public schools have an enormous amount of educational and financial resources for a small body of privileged pupils and that children in grammar schools have about twice as much money spent on their education as secondary-modern children. The same pattern affects higher education, where (as will be shown in the 1971 issue of *Social Trends*) the cost in 1969–70 of educating university students was £1284 per head, against £920 in colleges of education and £720 in advanced courses in further education. Under our present system, despite the recent advances, the average working-class child comes from a culturally and financially deprived home, has a relatively short and inferior school life and, if he reaches tertiary education, receives it on the cheap.

Despite the enormous weight of historical tradition and social injustice which educational reforms have had to combat, recent advances have taken deep enough root to prevent their total reversal by the present Government. At the very least, the view is no longer overtly expressed in responsible quarters that it is a waste of time providing education above elementary level for future industrial workers. Few will now be found to accept the Norwood insistence on 'types of mind', closely corresponding to social class and enunciated as recently as 1943. The reimposition of the old eleven-plus examination in its original form is no longer practical politics. But there has been a slowing down of comprehensive reorganization following Circular 10/70 (Department of Education and Science, 1970), Government approval of various forms of spurious reorganization, selection by new – and often more unfair – methods, and tax concessions aimed to benefit the clientele of the public schools. There has also been a marked reduction in educational welfare provision and planned expenditure at the secondary level, and expansion in higher education is likely to be held back. These reverses may well seem minor in the long run, but in what may be a long meantime, large numbers of children will suffer.

The first edition of *Education for Democracy* was conceived in part as an answer to the Black Papers. A more important purpose was to show how much remained to be done, not only in speeding up the necessary changes, but in altering the class-based nature of existing education. For the new circumstances of this second edition almost all the articles have been rewritten or brought up to date. An article by Les Brook on further education fills a serious gap in the first edition, and other new articles, by Wyn Williams and John Rennie, on social education, and Colin Stoneman, on the purpose and government of Colleges and Universities, are concerned in various ways to suggest methods of achieving more democracy and more democratic education.

Implicit in all the articles, old and new, is a set of ideas about the purpose of education and about the type of society we want. While our own views are not necessarily those of all our contributors, we believe that in general terms they share our approach. In our view, education and politics are inextricably linked. We cannot have a truly democratic society without a democratic education system, and the converse is also true. It is important to realize the difference between real and formal democracy, for in Britain democracy tends to be much more formal than real. For instance, the freedom of the press is of much more significance to those who own their own newspapers than to those millions who wished to read the many papers which were no longer profitable and hence failed to survive. (More papers have succumbed even in the two years since our first edition.)

In other fields, for instance industry, there is virtually no democracy at all, and it is commonly accepted that the existence of 'two sides of industry' is a fact of life. However, work is the most significant and creative part of almost everyone's life, and it is increasingly being realized that self-management is practicable. The thousands attending recent conferences of the Institute for Workers' Control and growing militancy in industry testify to an increased desire to exercise democracy where it matters most – in the workplace.

In a democratic society there would be no guarantee against making wrong decisions, and reason would not necessarily prevail at all times, for conflict between different groups would still exist. But reason would replace entrenchment, self-interested power and the enormous inertia of established institutions and conventional ways of behaviour as the main force in decision making. In so doing it would release people from the sense of powerlessness to influence events, even their own lives, which exists today, mainly in working-class people, but increasingly in others as well.

The relevance of these ideas to education should now be clear. We want more education for more people, leading to more democracy. We want an education system which is varied and flexible enough to develop fully all the different abilities and talents which children possess and want to use. These are value judgements and therefore not matters for argument. But our ways of striving towards this ideal (and indeed how far is it attainable) are certainly open to discussion. The articles in this book attempt to justify the following, amongst other things: nearly all children could benefit from the quality of education at present reserved for an elite at the public and grammar schools; most children could benefit from the abolition of streaming, rigid syllabuses and selection, and none need suffer; underprivileged children need special help if their talents and abilities are to develop to the full; all children could benefit from less authoritarian teaching and from learning in 'open' situations which give them a measure of autonomy; many more young people could benefit from some sort of higher education.

In both schools and higher education the use of examinations to grade people is anti-educational. The situation is even worse in universities than in schools, for there is no question of resitting exams to convert a third-class degree into an upper second. The degree classification is final, but all the unreliabilities and associated injustices of assessment remain. Fortunately, attitudes in this field are beginning to change, largely owing to student pressure. Dr Roy Cox, lecturer in university teaching methods at London University Institute of Education, has said that 'it is "intellectually dishonest" to add the results of, say, a dozen tutorial essays, two dissertations and four unseen three-hour papers and publish a single blanket classification' (*Observer*, 6 June 1971). There is a growing feeling among university lecturers that degree classes should be abolished altogether; if industry and the professional world really think they need their applicants graded, let them set their own examinations.

One may go on to ask if these proposed reforms in schools, colleges and universities are adequate, or whether the present divorce between 'education' and 'life' is artificial and should be ended. In recent years there has been an increasing tendency for older children to go outside the school walls and take part in the life of the community; Wyn Williams and John Rennie describe one such experiment in Nottingham. But there have also been suggestions of a more radical convergence of school and work. In both Cuba and China, for example, farm and factory-based schools are models worth studying. A number of writers, especially in the United States, have suggested that the years of formal schooling should be curtailed. Paul Goodman has suggested in an article in the *New York Review of Books* (10 April 1969) that 'education should be "tailor-made" according to each youth's developing interest and choice'. Such ideas are hardly new in England; in 'A factory as it might be' (1884), William Morris declared that

a factory will surely be a centre of education; any children who seem likely to develop gifts towards its special industry would gradually and without pain, amidst their book-learning be drawn into technical instructions which would bring them at last into a thorough apprenticeship for their own craft.

The introduction of such a completely new form of education would need to be made with care, particularly bearing in mind the aim of increasing the range of opportunities available to children rather than closing their options earlier, which could be an unintended result of an ill thought-out scheme. But it is at least worth considering whether what Paul Goodman calls 'the present extended tutelage [which] is against nature and arrests growth' should be with us forever.*

Nearly sixty years ago Bertrand Russell wrote:

Certain mental habits are commonly instilled by those who are engaged in educating: obedience and discipline, ruthlessness in the struggle for worldly success, contempt towards opposing groups, and an un-questioning credulity, a passive acceptance of the teacher's wisdom. All these habits are against life. . . . Contentment with the *status quo*, and subordination of the individual pupil to political aims, owing to indifference to the things of the mind, are the immediate causes of these evils; but beneath these causes there is one more fundamental, the fact that education is treated as a means of acquiring power over the pupil, not as a means of nourishing his own growth (*Principles of Social Reconstruction*, 1916).

Education and society have moved a long way since 1916. But it is still true that too little attempt is made to develop the individual pupil's capacity, that too much education is still 'against life'. We hope that this book will be seen as a contribution to creating an education system to serve a democratic society, as the older system served an unjust and unequal society.

We wish to acknowledge with gratitude the many individuals and institutions who have given us ready assistance in the preparation of this book, including the Department of Education and Science and our publisher, Jonathan Croall of Penguin Education. In particular we are most grateful for assistance over a prolonged period to John Hooton, of the University of Hull Institute of Education Library.

*For a fuller argument see Goodman's *Compulsory Miseducation*, *The Underachieving School* by John Holt and *School is Dead* by Everett Reimer, all published by Penguin in 1971.

# Part One
# **Controversy**

# Albert Rowe
## Human Beings, Class and Education

**Albert Rowe has taught in primary and secondary schools and in a college of education. He has been headmaster of four schools, ranging from a small country school to the David Lister High, a mixed comprehensive in Hull with 1400 pupils. He has lectured widely at educational conferences and in colleges and universities. He has also appeared frequently on television. He has written many books on English for secondary schools, articles and chapters on education in journals and books, and a book on teaching methods, entitled 'The Education of the Average Child' (1959). His latest book is 'The School as a Guidance Community' (1971).**

What I wish to propose here is a democratic view of human beings and education. Education in England has always been firmly tied to class, has reflected to an almost uncanny extent the assumptions the ruling classes held about themselves. The assumptions, too, which they held about other people and which, sadly but perhaps inevitably, others in their turn accepted. It was Mrs Alexander who unwittingly immortalized the position:

The rich man in his castle,
The poor man at his gate,
God made them, high or lowly,
And order'd their estate.

Hierarchal, elitist, establishmentarian, static, closed, anti-democratic – this was our society until recently. Birth, wealth, position, church membership, superior education were *of themselves* believed to confer personal worth and so privilege was unchallenged. Indeed it was the religionless ethic of the churches that provided one of the most potent justifications of that society, propping up the competitive capitalist *status quo* of the 'haves' by sanctifying profit making, promising compensatory pie in the sky to the 'have-nots' who did what they were told, and threatening retributory everlasting bonfire to those who didn't.

We can now smile at all this, but it's only within the last hundred years that we've progressed politically from an oligarchy through a paternalism to a potentially more open and more democratic society. 'Potentially', because the move towards a participatory society is now threatened by monolithic political parties and economic systems, and by the mass communications systems serving them, as well as by monolithic trade unions.

In education, only within the last two decades has some significant attempt been made to provide the kind of opportunities that a democracy ought in equity to provide for all its children, irrespective of family. First – for the sake of the individual – equality of educational opportunity. This, if the phrase is not to remain a comforting but empty shibboleth, would need to be based on a massive compensatory programme of housing, health and welfare, as everyone now knows. Second – for the sake of society itself – an education adequate in length, quality and democratic values to enable the future members of what one hopes will be a participatory democracy to fulfil in a true sense of community their responsibilities to one another and to the State.

The present attempt at democratizing education is now threatened by traditionalists, the self-appointed guardians of their own concept of academic excellence, who are busily attacking all those they label 'progressives', and by those worldly wisemen who believe only in the donkey-carrot-and-stick theory and who argue for doing nothing by saying that even were such a compensatory programme carried out, there would still be no equality of educational opportunity. True: the ideal is unattainable – the dice are too heavily loaded against too many. Yet this brute fact makes it all the more imperative, it seems to me, for democrats to go on striving to make it as much of a reality as possible. More idealism, not less, with its ability to inspire unselfish action, is needed today. Not Utopianism, for all Utopias, be they Platonic, theocratic, Jacobin, or communist, dehumanize man and end in tyranny. And certainly not more of the donkey-carrot-and-stick treatment, which is about all that is at present being proposed as the way out of troubles.

What the traditionalists are in fact seeking to do is to continue to monopolize quality education and keep it tied firmly to their own class. They know only too well what a winning wicket they're on, *for it is still as true today as it ever was that the most important predictors of a child's success are not his intelligence but his parents' class, the type of school he goes to, and the stream he's allocated to.* So if they succeed, they will reinforce what has throughout our educational history been a closed, self-perpetuating, self-justifying circle, a circle into which the children of 'the others' will still have little chance of breaking.

The thinking behind this approach, however its propagandists attempt to rationalize it, is based on a class view of human beings, a one-dimensional view, impoverished and impoverishing. The two kinds of education, quality and popular, are for two kinds of people, leaders and led, superior and inferior, the elite and the others. The elitist tradition has behind it a long history, culminating in the 1938 Spens Report (chairman, Will Spens, Rugby and Cambridge), which neatly divided pupils into three types – grammar, technical, modern. It based its division upon views of certain psychometricians (men more closely akin to soothsayers than scientists) that this could in fact be done, and proposed that the three types of pupils should be educated in three corresponding types of schools.

When at last the 1944 Education Act gave the chance to get away from tripartitism and educate pupils according to their age, ability and aptitude alone, the public school–Oxbridge power block seized upon what they wanted to hear, that is, the advice of the 1943 Norwood Report (chairman, Sir Cyril Norwood, Merchant Taylors and Oxford, headmaster in turn of Bristol Grammar, Marlborough and Harrow); and we were saddled with the inviolable talisman of the eleven-plus and its bitter and destructive aftermath – the creation of the secondary modern school, the school good enough for *other people's* children. Class separatism triumphant again.

These hierarchal, elitist, superiority–inferiority assumptions remain widespread and firmly embedded in our educational thinking and practice precisely because they are so deeply socially conditioned as to be unconscious. How else can the well-meaning but paternalist and patronizing 1963 Newsom Report (chairman, Mr, later Sir, John Newsom, Imperial Science College and Oxford), with its godlike invention of a new type of child, the 'Newsom', which it then promptly subdivided into three further types, Brown, Jones and Robinson, be explained? How else the 1968 Public Schools Commission recommendation – in effect that the taxpayer should pay for the abler offspring of 'the others' to be refashioned into public-school boys, thus presenting these schools with their eagerly desired brains-and-energy transfusion, and increasing and strengthening their output of young men who beyond argument *know* themselves, their accents, attitudes and life-styles to be superior? How else the action of most LEAs, Tory and Labour alike, of putting the label 'comprehensive' on systems in which grammar and comprehensive schools 'coexist' side by side, as if you can really have your cake and eat it. How else – if you still doubt that these assumptions are indeed unconscious – the Durham miners' determined rejection of comprehensive schools and support for what they genuinely believe to be 'our grammar schools'? How else the creation of the binary system in tertiary education, the real object of which is to preserve the myth that a degree from a university is better in some way (unspecified and unspecifiable) than a degree from any other kind of institution? Of – most Swiftean irony of all – the support the traditionalists' campaign is receiving from the very people whose children they would for ever exclude from quality education?

The 1959 Crowther Report gave irrefutable evidence of the great waste of academic ability, and potential and talent of all kinds: 'The report is about the education of English boys and girls aged from fifteen to eighteen. Most of them are not being educated.' So did the 1963 Robbins Report. 'Our investigations have suggested the existence of large reservoirs of untapped ability in the population.' And both stress that our society cannot achieve its twin aims of economic growth and higher cultural standards without making the most of the talents of its citizens.

Yet the problem of how to make the most of these talents, which is primarily the problem of how to prevent the wastage of working-class talents, is substantially no nearer being solved today. As J. W. B. Douglas and his colleagues point out (*All Our Future*, 1968) in what is by far the most significant educational research project undertaken in this country – eighteen years' continuous study of a representative sample of over 5000 children from birth on:

Middle-class pupils have retained, almost intact, their historic advantage over the manual working class. ... The social-class differences in educational opportunity which were considerable at the primary-school stage have increased at the secondary and extend now even to pupils of high ability. Thus nearly half the lower manual working-class pupils of high ability have left school before they are sixteen-and-a-half-years.

What drives these pupils (and so many others) out of the schools? I believe it is chiefly their unconscious acceptance of the upper-class assumptions I've been analysing. Assumptions embodied in the competitive and acquisitive ethic which are still accepted by the great majority of schools.

The fear of the traditionalists is that this ethic and its underlying assumptions will be abandoned: only by keeping it can they be sure of hanging on to their present class monopoly of quality education. So they are dressing the ethic in a new set of emperor's clothes.

Following in the footsteps of Spens, Norwood, Newsom and many predecessors, they would like you to think that their case has nothing to do with class, but rests on differences in intelligence and abilities so great that, especially at the upper end, they represent differences in kind, not degree. To parody *Animal Farm*, some animals are more equal than others, certainly, but a few are something different from, and far superior to, animals! So away with comprehensives and back to different kinds of schools for different kinds of children at eleven. Not only that – stream them in whatever school, the earlier the better. Then to make them work – you've got to *make* them work – see that they compete with each other. Use marks, publish mark lists, dish out rewards and punishments, promote them and demote them, send home reports which tell parents their year position and little else. All this is right because it truly reflects society itself. Isn't life a rat-race? And – the most revealing attitude – haven't we sweated and succeeded in the academic rat-race? So must they or go under, that's the way of the world. Don't we all live by competition and work because of the desire to acquire things?

They defend their brutalizing and stigmatizing strategies, which reject the majority and give them a sense of inferiority, of failure or partial failure, by claiming that they are necessary for the sake of that highly intelligent minority upon which the country depends, as it has always depended. But the only kind of intelligence they recognize is the one they narcissistically believe they've got a monopoly of. This is why they cry it up so and constantly try to oversell it.

The case against streaming I've made at length elsewhere.* All I need draw your attention to here is its central importance in the competitive ethic as the chosen instrument of the self-fulfilling prophecy. Label a child in school as C or D, expect only C or D performance, think and speak of him as a C or D child, persuade his parents to accept your labelling, and he will believe he is and act and achieve accordingly. Take the children who start out with great class advantages, label them A. . . . But I'm sure I needn't go on. And if final proof were needed that these assumptions are socially conditioned, it's to be found in the fact that streaming, still so common in primary and secondary schools as to justify it being called an educational system in miniature, is practised as rigidly by non-graduates as graduates, though themselves suffering from the label 'non-graduate and therefore inferior'. No wonder children – and not only working-class children – are driven out of such schools. For if school's a rat-race also, why stay to be losers when you know right from the start you'll lose? And if 'getting on' means 'getting up', you know as well as anyone that there isn't room at the top for you and so you're going to get out, opt out of the struggle to use your already labelled inferior talents to the full.

Is there a democratic way out of this anti-democratic impasse, this one-dimensional static view of human beings, overvaluing the few, devaluing all the others? I think there is.

*Where?, Supplement 12, 1968; The School as a Guidance Community, 1971.

We can make a start by removing those inequalities in our society which have been deliberately *institutionalized*; and nowhere more so than in education. For what is wrong with a society in which by your own efforts you can make your way to the top? Or, as those who are there (or think they are) are so fond of putting it: 'What's wrong with a society that produced me?' This makes explicit what I call The Great Tadpole Syndrome. The description of it which follows is Tawney's (*Equality*, 1931); and especially if we're successful we should give the lead in breaking out of it:

It is possible that intelligent tadpoles reconcile themselves to the inconveniences of their position, by reflecting that, although most of them will live and die as tadpoles and nothing more, the more fortunate of the species will one day shed their tails, distend their mouths and stomachs, hop nimbly on to dry land and croak addresses to their former friends on the virtues by means of which tadpoles of character and capacity can rise to be frogs.

We can begin at once in all schools to do away with such institutionalized inequalities as streaming and assigning the 'best' teachers and facilities to the 'best' pupils, and to replace the ethic of competition and acquisitiveness by one of cooperation and community. Impossibly idealistic? Impracticable? Not at all, for it is the ethic in the light of which an increasing number of us run our schools, schools successful as judged by the one criterion the traditionalists understand – examination passes; successful, also, in persuading increasing numbers of pupils of whatever class to stay on and educate themselves.

Our society needs intelligence and expertise, *but allied to a new democratic concern for others*. Not trained intellects alone, but *feeling intellects*, able in empathy to put ourselves in other people's shoes and act in the light of the knowledge that we are members one of another, and so treat others as they'd like to be treated. Of course we depend on the intellectuals, but equally we depend upon 'the others', upon their skills and qualities as human beings also.

This means that one has to take an optimistic, democratic view of all pupils, their nature and potentiality. It goes like this. Suppose that a sphere of a given size with innumerable different strands passing from the centre to the circumference represents the total potential – physical, emotional, intellectual – any one person could possess. Each strand represents a different specific capacity for excellence in all the manifold ways of being and becoming – in everything proper to a human being. The centre where all the strands begin represents the individual at birth. As he grows, he develops various strands to various lengths, but never all.

This is a multi-directional, multi-dimensional view of human nature, flexible enough to embrace life in all its infinite variety and richness. The prize of education is life itself. So the purpose of education must be to help each pupil to develop to maximum length as many strands of excellence as possible. For who can say which strands are most important in their ultimate contribution to the good and useful democratic life, to a democracy itself?

Leaving aside what a democratic society ought in conscience to do about the disadvantaged, which I've already touched upon, to put this view of human nature into practice one must create an *acceptable* school, a school which keeps the door of educational opportunity open to each pupil for as long as possible – until in fact he himself closes it. A school which gives each pupil an equal share of its resources – especially its best teachers – and waits to see what he can achieve, that is, encourages him later to 'select himself' for the various courses. In a word, a school which has broken out of the vicious circle of class-conditioned assumptions.

Such a school doesn't stream its pupils. It doesn't use competitive marks and mark lists, prizes and speech days. Marks never encouraged any pupils except those who got good ones, nor a prize any pupil except the one that was awarded it. Ought they to be used even for this? Surely the message is the wrong one – that the reward always lies outside the work and never in the work itself.

No prefects, either. In such a school pupils look after themselves and run their own affairs through committees, a true training in democratic participation. Its Parents Report gives first place to *self-measurement*, to how well each pupil is doing compared to his best self. No one can do better than his best, all that comparing him with someone else does is to make him unhappy, insecure and envious, a sure recipe for producing 'The Envious Society'.

Our behaviour is a function of our experience. If our experience is anti-democratic then so will be our behaviour. Change the experience and the behaviour will change. Schools which adopt an ethic of cooperation and community can create a milieu which is quickly accepted as natural and which will in time change class-biased assumptions into humane and democratic ones, accepted implicitly and unconsciously. A milieu in which all their pupils will grow, not only in brotherly awareness of one another as of equal ultimate worth, but also in generous and sensitive recognition of each other's valuable and infinitely varied qualities and gifts.

Only when schools put into practice this ethic, transform themselves into accepting rather than rejecting schools, will they stop producing 'tadpoles' and begin turning out human beings.

# Albert Hunt
## The Tyranny of Subjects

Albert Hunt taught English and French at Hamond's
Grammar School, Swaffham, Norfolk, for six years.
He became a part-time tutor for the Workers'
Educational Association and then moved to Shropshire
as area tutor organizer in Adult Education. He worked with
Peter Brook on 'US'. In 1965 he became the Director of
Complementary Studies at the Regional College of Art,
Bradford, and started a system based on project work and
student choice. One of the fruits of this was a re-enactment
of the Russian revolution in the streets of Bradford. He
has directed various productions and is currently theatre
critic of 'New Society'.

The young person in school is monstrously confronted by the
BARBARIAN in unforgettable form. The latter possesses almost limitless power. Equipped with pedagogical skills and many years of
experience he trains the pupil to become a prototype of himself. The
pupil learns everything required for getting ahead in the world – the
very same things that are necessary to getting ahead in school:
deceit, pretending to have knowledge one does not have, the ability
to get even without being punished for it, speedy acquisition of
clichés, flattery, subservience, a readiness to betray one's fellows to the
higher-ups. . . .

Bertolt Brecht

It is in fact nothing short of a miracle that the modern methods of
instruction have not yet entirely strangled the holy curiosity of inquiry. . . . I believe it would be possible to rob even a healthy beast of
prey of its voraciousness if it were possible, with the aid of a whip, to
force the beast to devour continuously, even when not hungry.

Albert Einstein

The world of play is necessarily one of uncertainty and discovery at every moment, whereas the ambition of the bureaucrat and the systems-builder is to deal only with foregone conclusions.

Marshall McLuhan

When I first joined the liberal studies section at the Bradford Regional College of Art, I knew precisely what I intended to do. I was going to teach film. For six years I had been doing this successfully as an adult tutor in Shropshire. I had taken films to village halls and evening institutes, shown them to groups and followed the viewing by discussion. The films had been carefully chosen to fit into a course: we had studied *The Un-American Cinema, Violence on the Screen, The Screen Hero*. The films had always provoked a direct response. Over a number of sessions we had built up a language of group analysis.

The idea of using film as the basis for liberal studies in an art college was logical. Film, which is both a visual and a dramatic medium, was half-way between the students' specialism (visual) and mine (literary). We would each, I thought, explore film from out of our own concerns and learn from each other.

To my surprise, I found that although most of the students enjoyed spending half a day each week looking at films, very few of them wanted to join in a serious discussion. If I wanted to involve the majority, I had to think up teaching techniques. I asked them to write an imaginary film script about a fairground and then showed them Lindsay Anderson's *O Dreamland* which he made in Margate funfair; I invited them to act out sequences, or turn them into radio tapes; once we used a film as evidence in a trial.

But as I ran out of ideas I began to feel irritated. Why should I have to use gimmicks to get them involved? Weren't they *serious*? Couldn't they see that film was self-evidently a good subject for them to study?

Some of them felt irritated too. Couldn't I see that if they were in the middle of a design, they might not want to waste an afternoon looking at films? Why should they have to spend an afternoon with me instead of getting on with their *serious* work?

Since we got on well together, the situation never turned into warfare. I turned a blind eye if they didn't turn up; they humoured me by joining in desultory talk about films.

But it was very frustrating and wasteful. It reminded me of every school situation I'd ever been in, both as pupil and teacher.

I might have been less aware of the frustration if I hadn't at the same time been involved in a totally different work situation elsewhere.

About a year earlier I'd been asked to produce John Arden's *Ars Longa Vita Brevis* in Shrewsbury. The play is built around children's games, and I'd simply invited students from Shrewsbury Art School to come and work on it if they were interested. We started by playing games and went on playing for several weeks, eventually bringing games and script together. But after the production we decided we wanted to go on working together.

We worked together, at weekends and in the holidays, for another year. We worked anywhere – in bed-sitters, rooms over pubs, once in the garage of a semi-detached on the ring road. We improvised a new story with the Ardens. We made plays for ourselves out of Boccaccio and Cervantes. Eventually, we embarked on a full-length production – *The Happy Haven*. We developed new working methods: two players would work together on an improvisation based on a scene and then show what they had produced to the rest of the group, who would analyse and make suggestions. From the improvisations, we worked back to the tight lines of the script, learning in the process the necessity of each line. One student became an expert on masks; another learned how to light the stage. The students invented their own costumes from anything that came to hand. They made their own props – mainly cardboard cut-outs. But the result was a complete unity of style simply because it had grown out of collective work, discussion and self-criticism.

We learned a great deal from this work. In the first place we learned a lot about the theatre. Our discussions and research ranged over Shakespeare, music-hall, Brecht, alienation – not because we wanted to improve or air our knowledge, but because these subjects suggested practical solutions to working problems.

Secondly, we learned a great deal about the discipline of language. We learned this in struggling through our own loose, haphazard improvisations to the line-by-line precision of the playwright. And at the same time we were engaged in the search for a theatre language through which we could communicate to an audience.

Thirdly, we developed our own form of critical analysis. We tested our own work together at every point and we brought in outsiders from time to time to test their reactions. In this sense the work, although apparently anarchic in organization, created its own discipline.

But above all we learned that it was possible to create a situation in which people's imaginative and intellectual energies could suddenly be released. We discovered potentialities in ourselves and in each other which we had never imagined to be there. The Hornsey students were to make the same discovery.

I was, therefore, working in contradictory situations. On the one hand at Bradford I was trying to teach a subject, Film, and was meeting with frustration; on the other hand at Shrewsbury we were working freely as a group who had come together around a common interest. But of the two situations, the one at Bradford was nearer to the educational norm.

The Bradford situation had grown out of two assumptions: first, that education should be *compulsory*; and second, that there are certain subjects which are, self-evidently, 'good' for people to learn. These assumptions lie at the heart of our educational system.

When the child is very young he acquires simple skills as part of a total experience. He hears other people around him talking and begins to form words. He learns through practice, in his own time and in his own way, how to make one foot follow another. Later, in his play, he adds new techniques as he needs them. His learning is a natural part of his everyday life.

At the age of five, he is drafted into an institution. At first, this institution may seem to be like the situation he has already experienced. He will be given materials and allowed to develop skills through play. But at a certain point, the institution will intervene. For part of the 'body of knowledge' that is common ground is the certainty that it is 'normal' for children to be able to read by a particular age.

At this point the child is introduced to his first subject – reading. Until then, he has been acquiring skills. A skill is a useful technique; you acquire it when you need it for a tangible purpose. A subject is something educational tradition says you ought to learn whether it is immediately useful or not.

You may have reached the stage where you want to learn to read. You are tired of having to ask other people to tell you what the balloons in the comics say. And so you are eager to learn. But on the other hand you may have quite different interests. You may be too busy drawing, or inventing new games, or learning to play draughts. But the system says that in either case you are now at the age where you *ought* to read.

Moreover, the material you are given to read – the tools you learn with – are very often completely divorced from any possible reason for *wanting* to learn to read. You are wondering what Batman said to Robin. You are given a book with pictures that show a boy in dark trousers, Persil-white shirt and neat tie; a girl in an equally white dress with a yellow cardigan and a white bow in her carefully brushed yellow hair; and a docile retriever on a lead. 'Here is Peter,' you read. 'Here is Jane. Here is the dog. The dog likes Jane. Jane likes the dog, and Peter likes the dog.'

Reading has become a subject You see it as 'work', something separate from your normal play activities. Soon, other subjects are added. By the time you reach secondary school, you are confronted with a bewildering array of them. They take up most of your day and they tend to come at you in forty-minute slabs. You are expected to be equally interested in all of them. But not too interested because soon the bell will go: 'Put your books away and get ready for the next lesson.'

At the end of five years, if you collect enough certificates, you will be recognized as an educational success. But what will you really have learned?

Taking into account all the time, effort, tension, persuasion and occasional violence, you will have learned very little about any of these subjects. Like Kingsley Amis I had a very good academic education. I went to a good grammar school, won a state scholarship and took a second-class honours degree in French at Oxford. At school, I spent many hours of at best boredom and at worst misery learning about mathematics, chemistry, physics and geography. And now I can't solve a quadratic equation, state Boyle's law or prove Pythagoras. I can just recognize a U-shaped valley. In the sixth form I learned how to write essays in thirty-five minutes and how to use quotations. When I went to France *after* taking my degree, I found I had to learn to speak and listen. Yet *I* was one of the school's academic successes.

If the pupils are not learning much about subjects, what *are* they learning in schools?

From a very early age the child becomes part of a pattern he never fully understands and is powerless to change. It is a pattern that is made up of rituals – of form periods, morning assemblies, lessons that follow each other in quick succession for no apparent reason, bells rung by other people that govern his changes of activity, milk, school dinners, homework. His life is part of a scheme that has been devised by people he does not know, and into which he is expected to fit without question.

And it is here that we come to the real content of our educational structure. At school, the child is taught by experience that it is normal for other people to organize his life. He will be told in Civics or History that he lives in a democracy, which means that people govern themselves. But he will *know* as an experienced fact that he must expect to be governed by other people who know better than he does.

Eventually he learns that the easiest way through school is to cooperate with the system. He emerges fully trained in the idea that it is his job to fit into the situation *as it exists* – and never to imagine that he might be capable of changing anything.

The educational system has, in fact, become the reflection of a society which gives the appearance of choice, but in which all the major decisions (from the devaluation of the pound to the manufacture of the H-bomb) are taken in secret by experts without consultation, a society which, in Marshall McLuhan's terms, deals 'only with foregone conclusions'.

But is there any alternative? At Bradford Art College, we took the situation into our own hands.

We began by abolishing the liberal-studies syllabus, the weekly liberal-studies timetable and the lecture courses built round subjects. Instead, we offered a programme of projects. Each project was to last a fortnight – we made an agreement with the departments that they would release students to us for one fortnight each year. There was a very wide choice of projects: in the beginning we started from our own enthusiasms, bearing in mind the need to find a topic which would interest enough students to form a working group. Later, the students began suggesting projects themselves.

Students were free to choose which project they wanted. The result was that we got on each project a cross-section of students from all years and all departments. Students worked together who otherwise would never have done so.

In this situation, the role of the teacher was changed. He became partly a catalyst generating projects and ideas, partly a personal adviser to individual students and partly someone whose particular expertise could be called on if it were needed in a project. We also used a lot of people from outside – local trades unionists, ex-RAF men (during a project on the bombing of Dresden), the pastor of a local gospel church, the secretary of the Council House Tenants' Association. People outside the college were thus involved in our activities. The barriers between college and locality were at least dented.

The projects generated their own energies and disciplines. Groups continued to work together long after the projects were over. A theatre group like the one in Shrewsbury was formed; other students made their own poetry group, not only writing poems, but hiring rooms, advertising their own readings, screen printing their poem posters. Others have made films or produced weekly newspapers. Some have developed advanced academic interests – one student who had repeatedly failed O-level English has worked his way through Baudelaire, Rimbaud, Lautréamont, Apollinaire (and picked up O-level in the process); another has produced a piece of original research about the structure of the textile industry.

The central factor in this programme is the shift from an externally imposed order, based on the sacredness of subjects, to a situation in which both teachers and students are free to make decisions – and to find areas of common interest which they can explore together.

How far could such a system be extended? It would, no doubt, be administratively complicated. But it would be a lot less complicated than the average comprehensive-school timetable. A few schools are already experimenting in similar directions.

But the tyranny of subjects is still firmly established. It can only be broken when those teachers who want to escape from it begin to realize their own capabilities.

For they, too, can act to gain control over their own lives.

# Anthony Arblaster
## Education and Ideology

**Anthony Arblaster was on the staff of 'Tribune' from 1965 to 1968. He then taught in the Philosophy Department at Manchester University for two years, and since 1970 has been a lecturer in politics at Sheffield University. He has contributed to 'The Socialist Register' (1970 and 1971), and was co-editor with Steven Lukes of 'The Good Society' (1971), a book of readings in political and social thought.**

It is striking how little of the abundant public discussion of education in the past decade has been concerned with the content of education, with *what* should be studied rather than with how, where, when and by whom. The long fight over comprehensive secondary education and virtually all the discussion and activity provoked by the series of official reports – Plowden on primary, Newsom on secondary and Robbins on higher education – revolved around questions of organization and structure, principles of selection, equality of opportunity, numerical expansion, standards of teaching and accommodation, and so on.

No comparable debate about the content of education took place. A general complacency prevailed. If the academics themselves were willing to discuss the matter, it was mostly in the way that they are always willing to discuss any topic, urgent or abstruse, in a detached and leisurely manner, safe in the knowledge that debate will almost certainly not lead to action.

In so far as the situation has changed in the past few years, this is primarily due, not to any official stimulus, still less to any sudden wave of self-examination or experimentalism on the part of academics, but to that much-maligned, much-disliked group, the students. To the irritation and embarrassment of many of their mentors, some of them have been doing exactly what education – on one interpretation – is supposed to encourage them to do. They have been asking awkward questions. And they have been asking about the content of the education that has been handed down to them, among other things. Why must we study Anglo-Saxon literature? Why does academic psychology ignore Freud? Why do we not learn Chinese history? Once begun, the questions and perplexities are endless.

As soon as such questions are raised, whatever the intentions of the questioners may be, ideological issues are brought into the discussion. For, whether it be the result of deliberate planning or of historical drift and inertia, the content of our education is determined by what people have thought to be the purposes of education, and those purposes can never be socially or politically neutral.

Thus for centuries British education was overwhelmingly the privilege of a social elite and had, essentially, the purpose of sustaining the superiority of the elite whereas the great mass of the people remained illiterate. The continuing power of this tradition is exemplified not only by such institutions as the so-called 'public' schools and the aristocratic rites and customs of the Oxbridge colleges, but also by their curricula. Then industrialization imposed new demands, and the notion of education as essentially a 'training' for a job and a particular social situation in life developed, and that too has made a lasting impression on British education. More recently, a more streamlined version of this crude utilitarianism has emerged. It is the concept of education as an 'investment', as a subservient part of the economy. Talent must be sought out and encouraged in order that it may be harnessed to the great national drive for higher production and bigger exports. This crassly money-minded approach (education 'pays') was rightly associated with the Wilson government's programme for modernizing British Capitalism, but it has become a consensus doctrine, accepted as obviously reasonable by everyone except 'doctrinaire' Socialists on the Left and old-fashioned high Tories on the Right.

It is perfectly clear that all these three approaches to education are ideological. They agree in subordinating education to the requirements of society and, more specifically, in seeing it as a means of sustaining and reinforcing the existing social and economic order. That is why they are now being challenged, and not before time. The high priests of British education, the vice-chancellors and the like who address conferences called to discuss the principles and purposes of education, have for the most part accepted without a murmur the increasing subordination of education to the requirements of business and industry, through the establishment of business schools, marketing and management studies, and the rest. Now it is they who complain that others are 'trouble makers', introducing political considerations into the hitherto supposedly inviolate sphere of education. The sky above our universities is dark with the wings of chickens coming home to roost.

It is not only the overall pattern of what is studied that has been, and continues to be, shaped by ideological pressures and assumptions. The shape of individual areas of study and the manner in which they are taught have been moulded in a similar way. This is most easily perceived in the human and social studies. There are, for example, clearly conservative implications in the basic assumption on which so much of contemporary linguistic philosophy is founded: that the job of the philosopher is not to invent new concepts or theories but simply to describe and analyse existing usages. To Professor J. L. Austin it seemed obvious that

our common stock of words embodies all the distinctions men have found worth drawing, and the connexions they have found worth marking, in the lifetimes of many generations: these surely are likely to be more numerous, more sound ... and more subtle ... than any that you or I are likely to think up in our armchairs of an afternoon (*Proceedings of the Aristotelian Society*, 1956–7).

To others of us it is at least equally reasonable to think that new and unfamiliar experiences or ways of seeing the world and human nature may require the formulation of new concepts and new theories, rather than efforts to cram them into old and established categories. Yet it has been left to 'outsiders' like Ernest Gellner (in *Words and Things*, 1959) and Herbert Marcuse (in *One-Dimensional Man*, 1964) to expose the conservatism of the linguistic orthodoxy in philosophy; and their criticisms have generally been ignored or treated with patronage and contempt by the 'professionals' in the field.

As one would expect, ideological bias is even more apparent in the study of politics where it infects even the definitions used. Politics itself is apt to be defined in terms of Western practice – 'competing interest groups' and so forth – and the same is true of less apparently neutral terms like freedom and democracy. In his widely known book, *Political Man* (1960), Seymour Martin Lipset produces a definition of democracy which is nothing more than a description of the American political system.

In history it is now acknowledged that the old Whig picture of England as

A land of settled government,
    A land of just and old renown,
        Where freedom slowly broadens down
From precedent to precedent

served a very convenient political function in the nineteenth century. But the approach to political history by which the Whig interpretation was partially discredited and superseded, that of Sir Lewis Namier and his followers and imitators, also had *its* ideological implications, and they were not radical either.

Examples could be multiplied – and have been, with varying degrees of conviction, by Robin Blackburn and Perry Anderson in their contributions to *Student Power* (1969). This kind of critique is a necessary work and must go on, though it goes on with a good deal more energy and success on the American side of the Atlantic than it does in Britain. It is important that we should penetrate the façades of false neutrality that lie behind them.

But having said so much, the awkward fact has to be faced that the most intractable difficulties connected with the inter-action of ideology and education have still to be grappled with. For example, what precisely is the objection of the Left to the types of ideological bias discussed above? Is it that they simul-taneously violate and masquerade as the objectivity which edu-cation should strive for? Or is it that the ideological bias of British education is not a radical bias, a bias to the Left? Is ideological bias avoidable, and ought it to be avoided?

These are very complex questions which require far more searching discussion than they can receive here. I shall offer only some (I hope) common-sense observations from which such a discussion might start.

There are areas of study in which it would not only be impossible but also undesirable to eliminate ideological bias. If the writings of Macaulay or Namier have their obvious political complexions, is that not also true of Tawney's *Religion and the Rise of Capitalism* (1926) and E. P. Thompson's *The Making of the English Working Class* (1963)? While not relaxing standards of honesty and objectivity, these writers too are concerned with the contemporary relevance of a certain interpretation of the past. We would not have it otherwise. For either Macaulay, Namier or Tawney to have aimed at a bias-less neutrality would not only have made their history dull; it would also have involved the sacrifice of what is most valuable in their work, the element of interpretation together with the insights which *only* such partial, partisan approaches can supply.

The reaching after an unattainable neutrality in the social and human studies generally produces only a narrow, cautious and unilluminating dreariness. Truth, not to say mental stimulation, is far more likely to be produced by the open conflict of different ideological approaches. What we have a right to demand is that such conflict should not only be tolerated but actually encouraged. Marxists ought not to be required to teach a Capitalist version of economics, nor should Socialists be expected to accept the Western liberal interpretation of the study of politics. Professors ought not to have the power to pack departments with teachers of one ideological persuasion alone.

Open ideological conflict within education would also help to undermine those false claims to neutrality and objectivity, mentioned earlier, which so often serve to conceal a conservative bias. Again we should demand that ideological bias is overt, there to be identified and analysed. As a teacher of political theory with definite opinions of my own I try to maintain certain standards of fairness and objectivity, and also to avoid thrusting my own opinions upon students. But I know that I cannot hope to be absolutely neutral, and believe that the likelihood of provoking thought and interest would be reduced if I tried to be.

The honest course therefore seems to be to make my bias evident, so that others can discount it if they wish to or need to.

As has been suggested, there are those on the Left who complain that much existing education is indoctrination, but would be quite satisfied if Socialist indoctrination replaced Capitalist indoctrination. This seems to me an untenable, and, indeed, a deeply undemocratic attitude towards education. Difficult as it is to be precise about it, we should hold fast, none the less, to the distinction between education and indoctrination.

Many people of differing opinions, including, of course, those who would make education a tool of the economy, agree in seeing education as a process of imprinting certain ideas and values upon the impressionable minds and characters of the young. Once that principle is accepted, it is very difficult effectively to oppose those who are determined that education shall be a prop for the existing social and economic order, and who have the power and the money to ensure that it is so.

It is hardly an original thought, but I want to suggest once again that education, rightly understood, is not indoctrination of any kind, but an essentially critical activity. Its function is to encourage people to think independently, to doubt, to question, to investigate, to be sceptical and inquisitive. As such, it is, in any society, a subversive force. For this process of questioning and inquiring and debating is not to be channelled into areas of study which are remote and abstruse, and therefore politically 'safe'. It ought to be directed towards the most important and the most relevant issues in the society. So far from education reflecting the current consensus or 'conventional wisdom', those generally accepted notions are exactly the ones which an open and healthy system of education would be most concerned to scrutinize and query, whatever their political colour might be. Education should provide a permanent opposition to orthodoxies, both political and intellectual. Thus education does have a social function, but it is not a subservient one. It is essentially an independent and democratic function. Its task is not to *serve* business, government and the economy, but to examine, investigate and analyse them.

It is almost superfluous to say that although the idea of education as a critical activity is not dead, it is not the dominant force shaping British education today. It is itself, therefore, a critical concept by which we can measure, and oppose, the increasing subordination of the educational system to the demands of industry, business and the economy, and the domination and restriction of many fields of study by the complacent and narrow ideology of Western capitalism.

## Postscript

Having the opportunity to revise this article two years after it was written, I have made a few updating alterations. But what I find most depressing is that so little has changed, and so little progress has been made since it was first written. Here and there, mainly in response to student pressure, some intelligent revisions of curricula are being made. Here and there is greater flexibility in relations between the entrenched empires of academic interests and departments. But the general lack of movement, or even debate, continues, providing abundant evidence of the lethargy and sterility of those chiefly responsible for the overall pattern of tertiary education in Britain.

The prospects for an increase in ideological tolerance within education in the immediate future are not particularly bright either. In the long term it will prove impossible to exclude radicals, for there are too many of them. But in the short term there can be no doubt that many powerful people in the academic world will continue to use their power to discriminate against staff and students who challenge the established ideology and structure of educational institutions. However, the Council for Academic Freedom and Democracy, founded in 1970, is one institution (or counter-institution) which should make it less likely that such partisan abuses of educational power go unchecked and unchallenged in future. Significantly, in view of the title of this book, it is the word 'democracy' which identifies the Council's independent and radical position. Every teacher and academic pays lip service to something called 'academic freedom', but it is only the radicals who recognize that both its preservation *and* its extension are dependent upon the democratization of education institutions. Democracy *in* education is the prerequisite of education *for* democracy, and of the ideological openness for which I have argued.

# Michael Duane
## Education in Britain Today

**Michael Duane was for six years headmaster of Risinghill Comprehensive School, London, the closing of which in 1965 led to prolonged controversy. He is now honorary principal lecturer at Garnett College, London, and speaks very frequently to gatherings of students, parents, teachers and others. He has written many articles and broadcasts on education, contributed to 'Education for the Seventies' (1970), is part-author with A. S. Neill, Leila Berg and others of 'Children's Rights' (1971), and is slowly writing his own book on education as distinct from schooling.**

Since man is born not, like the ant, equipped with the habits and skills necessary for survival, but culturally 'plastic', he has to be educated into the particular bodies of knowledge, the skills, the values and the personal and group relationships that different peoples have found useful for survival in widely different geographical and climatic conditions. The more sophisticated the culture and the larger the human group, the more the individual has to learn and the longer the period he will spend in being educated before being accepted as a fully productive adult.

Every system of education, in whatever country, will, therefore, reflect in detail the predominant values, assumptions and social relationships characteristic of its parent society. Britain is no exception. Further, contradictions in the parent society – progressive stirrings alongside traditional modes of thought and functioning – will find their counterparts in that system. To the extent that society allocates different social tasks to different groups, these groups will receive the type of education appropriate to their social function.

The tendency of every education system is, therefore, to pe petuate the existing form of its parent society, or rather, the form of that society as it existed a generation or two previously, since the sources of the teachers' educational material lie both in their own earlier experiences (it is principally the older generation of teachers who dictate and maintain policy), and in the textbooks that tend to reflect situations and subject matter already out of date.

The central drive in British as in the rest of Western mass-production society is to protect and increase wealth for the owners of wealth, but the techniques for doing this have changed considerably and brought corresponding changes in the structure of society during the last two hundred years. The rapid expansion of scientific knowledge, and of the application of scientific principles to the means whereby we produce and distribute goods, has made it important for the owners of property not only to own wealth but also to understand how it can be increased. It has also made it necessary for them, first, to buy for their sons an education in the technical knowledge essential if they are to retain control of that wealth under more complex conditions; second, to encourage the growth of those older professions (law, the Services, teaching, medicine) and the newer professions (finance, advertising, journalism, engineering, communications, etc.) equally essential to the protection and the increase of wealth.

### The public schools

The wealthy have, therefore, educated their young under the most intensive conditions possible, namely, the secluded boarding school, staffed by some of the best products of Oxbridge, taught in very small groups to ensure a maximum of individual attention with equipment and in buildings, often provided by lavish gifts from industry, that are amongst the best in the country. Such an education, under conditions that minimize familial and other 'distractions' and maximize the emotional relations between teacher and taught, gives their products a deeply rooted attachment to certain concepts. These include their right to own property and to form the ruling class in a system of parliamentary government, strongly felt views about the forms of dress and behaviour that are the outward signs of their social-class unity, considerable intellectual capacity, and an ability to take responsibility and make decisions in those areas that affect their personal and social lives, as in politics, business and the management of industry.

It is common to decry or ridicule the rituals and the eccentricities of behaviour and dress in public schools. We now understand, however, that their effect is to create multiple bonds of fellow-feeling, of empathy and, above all, of close identity of valuations among those who are submitted to these experiences. The creation of similar bonds is practised universally wherever an elite or corps of members is required within a society to perform functions essential to the preservation of the ruling class. Instances include the corps of Spartan warriors, the groups of medieval knights, the Japanese Samurai, the Prussian officer caste and the SS corps of Hitler Germany. The strength of the emotional bonds created by their training makes for such cohesion and readiness of communication that such elites are able to maintain power over much larger classes and groups within the same society.

These bonds of feeling and value have the further effect that they insulate the individual against the effects of personal guilt for repressive action against lower class groups or individuals. As capitalist industry has come to depend more and more on specialist skills the committee has evolved as a means of harmonizing diverse forms of knowledge and experience for production. It has also developed the useful function of removing the burden of decision from individuals when such decisions may be wrong, or may clash with the moral code of the individual in his relations with others, or when the decisions are likely to cause or increase disaffection among workers.

## The grammar schools

From their early but limited tasks of preparing the sons of the gentry to administer the country and the clever sons of the poorer classes to enter the Church, the grammar schools increased and developed at the end of the nineteenth and in the early years of the twentieth century. Their new function was to educate the rapidly increasing numbers required by the growth of the older professions and the new sciences and semi-professions now fully accepted as necessary to protect and increase wealth in a society no longer pastoral and agricultural. Although for a long time hampered by traditions associated with the teaching of the 'classics', they have, more recently, included mathematics and the sciences. Their whole curriculum is now, in fact, carefully built to prepare their pupils for their adult roles in the middle class as initiators, developers and communicators of ide  Ancillary purposes are the development of respect for property, for law and for organized religion – all ideas held to be conducive to the stabilization of social relationships.

By their very function these schools offer to their pupils the possibility of success through participation in control and decision. Their most promising pupils go on to the university; the less promising occupy the lower ranks of the technically minded lower-middle class – the bank clerks, the technicians, the sellers of advertising space. Many tend to become so engrossed with the values and the minutiae of their own particular skill and to identify so fully with the purposes of their employers that they are unable to lift their eyes to the possibility of cooperation for the benefit of the whole society. Their sense of alienation is no less marked than that of the factory worker, because they neither own nor control the institutions within which they operate and (with the exception, perhaps, of creative artists) can rarely exercise their specific skills outside those institutions.

The grammar schools, like the public schools, have been associated with particular forms of dress – caps, blazers, gym slips, scarves – and with particular forms of behaviour such as religious assemblies, team games, etc., though to a much less intense degree. Strenuous efforts have always been made, and still are today, to create within the grammar school the ethos of the public school, but because they are almost entirely day schools, the efforts to establish a secondary elite have never been so successful as in the public schools, though successful enough to keep a large majority basically Conservative or at most Liberal in their politics.

Since their curricula are designed to equip their pupils for entry to the universities and the professions and since they are populated by children of mainly non-manual and professional workers, most of their pupils are already saturated with middle-class values relating to religion, the law, property and the virtues of free enterprise, though an increasing number seem to be less sure in these convictions.

## The secondary modern schools

For the working class, education was, until recently, fairly simple. The 1870 Education Act set out to equip them with an elementary knowledge of reading, writing and reckoning adequate to man the shops, offices and factories of an expanding industry. It also set out to impress habits of industry, sobriety and a respect for authority such as would obviate any resurgence of early nineteenth-century revolutionary enthusiasms.

The inadequacy of this concept of education for the world of the Apollo space missions and for the internationalism implied in communications satellites is reflected in the discontent with 'selection at eleven-plus', in the growth of demands for comprehensive education, in continued industrial strife, and in the difficulty that we find in competing with our younger and more technically conscious rivals abroad. Our failure to use science and technology in planning is of such a kind that very many of the social and material benefits accruing to this country during the last fifty years have come about, not as a result of consciously planned reseach directed to these ends, but as a 'spin-off' from research into ways of improving our powers of defence and aggression.

The failure of successive Labour governments to find solutions to urgent social problems of full employment, housing, comprehensive education and work democracy has perpetuated many of the worst features of working-class life. Some of these are (a) the alienation that is seen as a sense of powerlessness and purposelessness so great as to prevent organization to secure the improvement of working conditions; (b) the maintenance of culture at a dispiritingly low level through continued low standards of living; (c) the creation of divisions within the working class, seen in such events as demarcation disputes; (d) the denial of any meaningful participation by the working class in control over the nature, purposes and uses of their work, and the consequent reinforcement of their view that the freer aspects of modern education have for them little relevance.

Efforts to break away from the interlocking strangleholds of low social class and poor education by the establishment of basic freedoms from poverty and disease in the Welfare State and by the drive for comprehensive education are proving much more difficult to realize than anticipated. Too little account has been taken of the deep-rooted character structures inculcated by the older modes of life. Moreover, there has been a continuance in new social forms, such as the Department of Health and Social Security and many comprehensive schools, of behaviour and motivation associated with 'charity' to the lower orders in the former, and elitist attitudes and hierarchies in the latter.

Post-war research has confirmed the common-sense view that the public schools are populated by children of the upper-middle class and the landed aristocracy; grammar schools by the middle class and a disproportionately small number from the children of manual workers; and secondary modern schools by the children of the working class. It has been clearly shown that the claim to offer 'equal educational opportunity for all children' is a myth. It has shown, above all, that parental interest in the child's progress, parental education, income and size of family are crucially important in ensuring entry to higher secondary and university education.

The discrepancy between the quality of the education provided in grammar schools and that provided in secondary modern schools – in terms of staff–pupil ratios, teacher qualifications and average levels of salaries – is maintained, in spite of popular demand for grammar-school education by a majority of parents questioned, by devices built into the Burnham Agreement which controls the staffing of schools and the salaries of teachers.

The staffing of a school and the salary of the Head are determined, not, as might be thought, by the number of pupils but by the number of Burnham Units the school can accommodate. Pupils up to the age of thirteen count as one-and-a-half Burnham Units; pupils of thirteen plus count as two; those of fifteen plus as four; those of sixteen plus as six and those of seventeen plus as ten.

The vast majority of pupils in modern schools leave between

the ages of fifteen and sixteen, whereas in grammar schools almost all children stay to sixteen to take O-levels and over 50 per cent stay on to take A-levels. Thus the older pupils build up a much larger total of Burnham Units and the result is that staff–pupil ratios are about 15 per cent more favourable to grammar schools than to secondary modern schools. Common sense might have supposed that children of lower academic ability and coming from culturally poorer homes would need more teachers than those in the top 25 per cent of the ability range. Basil Bernstein comes to a similar conclusion in suggesting ways of overcoming linguistic deficiencies resulting from social-class conditioning.

Further, as additions to the basic salary of teachers are made for the possession of a degree or its equivalent and for the exercise of special responsibility (historically associated with the teaching of academic subjects to higher levels), grammar-school teachers receive a much higher average salary than secondary-modern school teachers. Seventy-five per cent of grammar-school teachers in full-time service are graduates but only 16 per cent of secondary-modern school teachers are so qualified. Over all, these differences, together with the longer school life of the grammar-school pupil and the greater cost of his books and equipment, mean that the cost of educating the average grammar-school pupil must be about twice that for the average secondary-modern school pupil.

Surveys of the social-class background of teachers show that the higher the social position of the school (in terms of the social background of the pupils), the higher the social background of the teachers, so that the public schools contain the highest proportion of teachers from the upper levels of the professional and managerial class; while secondary modern schools have the highest proportion from the lower-middle class and the skilled manual worker section of the working class. It also appears that where the social-class backgrounds of teachers and pupils most nearly coincide, as in public schools and direct grant grammar schools, disciplinary problems are fewest; but where they diverge widely, as in secondary modern schools or in grammar schools situated in lower-working class areas, they are most frequent.

## The comprehensive schools

On the evidence generally available, comprehensive schools still base themselves on traditional patterns of organization, staff relationships and salary structures. They have mostly been built by architects operating within conventional ideas of the function of education (and very closely tied to cost limits set by the Department of Education and Science), and they are staffed by teachers of whom a majority have neither training nor experience of the kind to help them think differently. Nevertheless, within comprehensive schools throughout the country, there *is* a new thinking about curricula, organization, staff–pupil relationships and, especially interesting, about relationships between the school, the parents and the outside world. The old impression of obsession with religious instruction, with the niceties of fine streaming, with uniforms, prefects and competition – all characteristic of traditional schools – are steadily giving way to more rational preoccupations.

The relative failure of the comprehensive schools to achieve, to date, more than marginal improvement on the tripartite system highlights research (by Bernstein *et al.*) that shows how middle-class parents systematically structure the attitudes of their young towards the use of language as an important perceptual and conceptual tool, and towards academic achievement as a means towards social advancement; and how, in so doing, they give their children a long start in the competition for places in higher education and in middle-class careers. From the facts of this research it follows that the larger classes, the academic curricula and the irrelevant training of secondary-modern school teachers conspire to reinforce the alienation, the feeling of apathy towards education seen in so many working-class children despite the efforts of sensitive teachers to make their work the personal, illuminating and rewarding experience that it should be for their pupils. We see that by the time children start in the comprehensive school their levels of achievement have been almost completely determined by the home and have been reinforced by the primary school, so that they arrive with widely differing intellectual capacities and ambitions and are streamed accordingly for even more intensive reinforcement of their existing state.

## Further and higher education

It follows from what has already been said that we find in further and higher education class and functional divisions similar to those in the secondary field. As the Robbins and the Crowther Reports showed, the higher social classes predominate in Oxbridge and the proportion of manual working-class students increases as you move 'down' the educational spectrum towards the technical college and the local college of further education.

In all this the development of language is crucial. Speech and thought – especially the detailed and complex thought required to establish communication, to control the multifarious systems and processes of modern industry and to devise new materials, processes and organizations – is the one activity that distinguishes man from animals. It is in this central activity that resides man's power to survive. The class system, and the schools that operate within and for that system, develop high levels of speech and thought for the upper strata of society and effectively deprive the lower strata of this power-giving function.

For too long we have, in this country, promulgated the myth that our education system is actuated by Christian, democratic and humanitarian principles. The facts elicited by a growing body of evidence suggests that it is rather a systematically ruthless conditioning of children for adult roles geared to the production of material wealth for a section of our society, rather than for the extension of civilized standards to all.

# Part Two
## Background

# Nicholas Tucker
# The Underprivileged Child in the Underprivileged Area

Nicholas Tucker has taught in comprehensive schools
and worked for five years as an educational psychologist
before taking up his present post as lecturer in
Developmental Psychology at the University of Sussex.
He is the author of 'Understanding the Mass Media'
(1966) and has edited a Penguin Educational Special of
cartoons from 'The Times Educational Supplement'
('A Hundred of the Best', 1968). He has written articles
for 'New Society', 'Where?', 'The Times Literary
Supplement' and many other journals, mostly about
children and their imaginative responses.

More education! How many times has one read or been told in
the past that freedom of opportunity, the disappearance of prejudice and the revelation of latent talents would all be ours, one
day, if there could be more education. Perhaps we are a little
wiser today; recent research, notably the findings of the Plowden
Report, have suggested that what is needed, in deprived areas,
is not more education but education of a different type altogether. Some new ideas have since been tried, often with success,
and the policy of adopting Educational Priority Areas (EPAs)
has the support, however timid, of the Government and the
LEAs. But I sometimes wonder, when witnessing some of the
very high hopes – political and otherwise – that have surrounded
these new developments, whether many people are still pinning
too many hopes on education as *the* instrument of social change,
to the exclusion of other relevant social factors. How much can
school and after-school activities be fairly expected to achieve on
their own?

I worked for some time in a decaying area of London, typical in many of its problems of older run-down areas of most large towns. Often, I found myself thinking of the old joke about an American who asked whether the War against Poverty had been declared yet, as he personally was ready to surrender at any time. In fact, there is an element of reality in this; it was this feeling of surrender that characterized so many of the hardcore problem families I came across in schools and in a child guidance clinic. Of course, many families were doing better than ever before; but for those who were not coping often the only escape route left open to them was alcohol or petty crime. The admission rate to mental hospitals in this area was 77 per cent higher than the national average.

Many of these parents came from backgrounds even more hopeless than their present plight, which led one to wonder, in turn, about the likely fate of their own children. Would they reproduce the same old problems, perhaps slightly watered down through each generation, or would they be able to grow out of the situation altogether?

This was a worry that naturally affected many teachers too, especially in the primary schools, who often felt that they were merely standing by watching a child deteriorate, unable fundamentally to offer him very much real help. Part of my job was to explain to such teachers, often almost desperate in their anxieties about a child, that in most cases it was no good simply to think in terms of taking a child away from the family or general environment. Children's homes, special boarding schools, foster parents can very seldom offer a really adequate substitute for a home, except for a short time or in the most extreme cases. So often children tend, in the long run, to reject any attempt to transplant them, and at best the operation, to be successful, has to be performed with an extreme delicacy and timing impossible for most hard-pressed social agencies to achieve.

So on the whole the problem child must stay in his home and environment, propped up or not, as the case may be, by one of the social services. In fact in a deprived area, there is often a temptation amongst other authorities to foist upon the social services a hopelessly omnipotent role, as if all that needed to be done with a severe problem could be achieved by one interview with a psychiatrist or a child-care officer. In reality, any effective supportive therapy can take a very long time and even then may never really be able to counteract all the different forces working against a child or family.

The teacher, then, must cope as well as possible, sometimes with the most desperate situations, and although she may feel that she is not really helping that particular child, she often does more for him than anyone else could achieve. School, given the chance, can become a haven for an unhappy child, a place where he can live and grow in security; and we know from J. W. B. Douglas's *The Home and the School* (1964) that, in the very best primary schools, children whose parents show little interest in their work can do as well as those children who have full parental support.

But in deprived areas, are the schools given the chance to be among the very best, in response to what is obviously an overwhelming need? Certainly, the general recognition given to primary education by the Plowden Report has helped morale everywhere, but Assisted Travel Schemes to encourage teachers into difficult areas and the recognition of Educational Priority Area schools have hardly dented the problem. Extra financial inducements to teachers that have resulted are pitifully small; it is not really surprising that teacher turnover is still very high, and that head-teacher posts often have to be readvertised in order to attract enough good candidates.

And why don't the secondary schools get EPA treatment? A few of them, as it is, get far more than their fair share of really difficult pupils, and in this position of 'sink' schools (or 'crap' schools, in the local jargon) it obviously gets increasingly hard for them to get good staff – again, where the need is greatest. School inspectors who should bring that stimulus to the schools which is often automatically provided in middle-class areas by interested and informed parents, head teachers who should be fostering home–school relations and putting forward really creative schemes of work, and educational psychologists who should be helping with certain very difficult children over a long period of time are often so busy in poor areas keeping up with the minute-to-minute problems of their jobs, that there may never be enough time to get all these important things done. But the concept of an EPA implies extra work over the whole of the educational scene, not just within the schools; and other services linked with the schools should also be strengthened.

Even so, there is no doubt that in many deprived areas the primary schools, many of which have always been of a high standard, are still improving. Some voluntary schemes are now working within the schools, perhaps taking children out to explore their environment (this may need to be as basic as showing the younger children the way to the nearest recreation ground and, once there, how to use some of the apparatus). I do not feel, though, that the whole concept of an EPA school has been seen for what it really could be – a major reshaping of educational ideas and habits. The precedent has been established, however, and could develop in the future into something more significant.

But why tackle the schools alone in all this? An EPA implies exactly what it says: the whole social scene. There is a limit to what any one school can be expected to achieve single-handed when pupils are faced with the most monstrous social problems. And beyond the school, there is often not the sense of urgency one would hope for, with some social services almost acting as a mirror to the general sense of hopelessness, rather than offering a more positive antidote. Some children's departments, for example, have staff turnovers of almost epic proportions, watched sometimes rather cynically by the young people within their care. As in the schools, it is vitally important for children, often rejected at home, to have some sort of continuity with adults elsewhere, and not to have to suffer again and again the secondary rejection that goes with a constant change of personnel. Ideally, it should be *difficult* to get a job in the social services of a depressed area, not the sort of post one can just walk into with the very minimum of training, which sometimes happens now.

In my area essential provisions like youth clubs still tend to jog along very much as they always have, without very much time for the unclubbables who are, of course, a very considerable handful. The actual premises used are often quite insufficient for the needs of young adolescents, especially girls, who want something better than plain wooden floors, a tatty record-player and odd sticks of school furniture dotted around. Better, perhaps, to hang about the street corners, or the canal – a sour, undeveloped stretch of water – or else visit the local park, which is badly understaffed, and a prey to vandals who climb in every weekend at night to tear up flowers, throw benches into the lake and break into park-keepers' huts. Some adventure playgrounds could surely take up some of this energy, although efforts in this direction do not seem to have got very far.

Elsewhere in the area I know, there are some positive signs of change. Museums and children's libraries, for example, are beginning to adapt themselves towards the needs of young people, with some success. Private enterprise, however, is far less adventurous. There is not one bookshop – even a W. H. Smith – in an area serving over a quarter of a million people. The toyshops tend to sell cheap rubbish, at a time when we know how important some early stimulating material can be. There are no smart discotheques or dance halls, and over much of the area, night and day, hangs the stench of a local factory, making what must be either furniture polish or cosmetics.

All these details on their own may not seem that bad, but against a backdrop of mean council development, litter-ridden streets, and dirty, over-crowded old houses, the pervasive atmosphere is that of one huge dump; not perhaps to the older people, who remember it as it once was and still have the sense of community that is elsewhere disappearing. But in a small survey once made on how to improve the area, the overwhelming response was simply: it can't be improved, the only good thing to do is get out – if you can. Sure enough, the population continues to decline. Even so, many people continue to make the best of it, often by concentrating upon creature comforts perhaps as an antidote to the squalor outside. But for others without the money for this, the answer is often depressive apathy.

The ambitious 'Head Start' Scheme, tried in America as part of the War on Poverty project, was in many ways a most exciting idea, despite its teething troubles. Is it totally unrealistic to imagine us trying something of the same sort in a few of our own grey areas? Such a scheme would principally involve a massive injection of energy into the community, very much as the Notting Hill Trust has achieved in London on a smaller scale. In most deprived areas at the moment, there is simply not enough money or leadership to encourage and direct the local initiative which would surely come, given a reasonable start.

Why not, for example, introduce schemes for clearing rubbish and helping the old, theatre workshops, art studies, football coaching, mobile toyshops and bookshops, involvement in after-school activities, playgroups, adventure playgrounds, coffee-bar projects, amenity projects, neighbourhood projects? Of course, some work along these lines is already going on in different places, but organization, financial support and general facilities are needed on a much wider and more generous scale to make much of an impression.

All this in no sense need emerge as a middle-class takeover bid for the soul of the area. Rather, much of it would be offering the type of activity already enjoyed by children in good schools everywhere, and especially important for those who may particularly need this type of stimulus and support after school hours. In place of the apathy and drifting there would at least be something positive going on, organized wherever possible by local people with outside help and encouragement. Obviously many children, like their parents, will continue to drift into whatever scheme is put forward, but others who I feel are still fundamentally looking for a meaningful outlet for the long holiday and weekend hours may at last find one.

How to attract good applicants to work in deprived areas in this way remains to be seen. Good salaries would help, especially in those professions which have always been underpaid, and perhaps also assistance with housing. Also an atmosphere of experiment would surely be exciting to work in, especially if it were accompanied by essential provisions such as adolescent units and hostels, which at the moment are hard to find even in the prosperous areas, despite their importance.

In fact, imaginative appointments have already been made in some fairly new fields, such as adventure playgrounds, often with considerable success. Smaller local centres have done, and continue to do, amazingly creative work in the most barren of surroundings. Very often projects like these suffer principally from a shortage of cash, and can hardly pay their workers a living wage. Once again, more backing over a much wider scale is obviously needed, for if the EPA school is really going to help the underprivileged child, then it will need just this kind of support to take over where it leaves off. As Douglas reminds us in *The Home and the School*, a middle-class child with adverse home circumstances generally gets by at school much better than the working-class child with the same handicap, since the one tends to get the support from the environment denied to the other. This may be true of the past; need it always be true of the future?

## Postscript

Since the first edition of this book there has not been very much progress to report in this area. Teacher supply may be more adequate now, but elsewhere conditions in the underprivileged areas remain very much the same. Families who can, still tend to move out; those that remain are often relative newcomers who have drifted or been drafted to the area because of available cheap housing there – however substandard. Faced with an enormous case-load, the social services may be able to cope at an immediate level, but will often not have the time for the long-term supportive work that may be expensive in hours but still worthwhile to the extent of having any lasting effect.

Problems that may have been building up for generations – in families or even in whole urban areas – cannot be solved quickly or easily. Nor can they really be tackled by taking just one aspect of the situation and ignoring all the other linked variables. Interesting schemes for total community involvement continue to develop, with local authority or Home Office backing, but in a national sense this sort of development is still sporadic, piece-meal and ludicrously under-financed. If we really want to shift some of our social problems, it is going to take far more resources and time than anyone has yet dreamed of in official circles. But if these problem areas continue to be largely ignored, in the sense of any *significant* effort for change, then there seems to me a risk that one day they will have become so depressed that rehabilitation may be an impossibility. 'It's the good will of the prisoners that keeps the place alive', said Richard Neville, the editor of *Oz*, after leaving Wormwood Scrubs. I feel very much that this is true of the underprivileged areas. Many of the people living there do still manage to cope under the most depressing social circumstances. But no one should gamble upon this type of acceptance lasting indefinitely.

# Ken Coates and Richard Silburn
## Education in Poverty

Ken Coates is tutor in sociology in the Department of Adult
Education at Nottingham University. Richard Silburn is
lecturer in Applied Social Science at Nottingham University.
They are co-authors of 'Poverty, Deprivation and Morale'
(the 'St Ann's Study', 1968), 'The Morale of the Poor'
(1968) and 'Poverty: The Forgotten Englishmen' (1970).
Ken Coates is the editor of the 'Spokesman'.

With the publication of the Plowden Report in 1967, poverty was
rediscovered for the administrators of English education. This
is something to be grateful for; the overwhelming complacency
of the 1950s at last gave place to a measure of sombre realism.
As recently as 1959, the Crowther Report enthused about 'how
sharply the average standard of living has risen', and insisted
that full employment, taken together with 'the combined effect
of inflation, of progressive taxation and of the social security
schemes of the welfare state has been [able] to direct the larger
part of the rise in the national standard of consumption to the
lower-income groups'.

Against this comfortable view Plowden maintained, 'there has
not been any appreciable narrowing of the gap between the least
well-off and the rest of the population'. At least this last assessment places its authors in the real world, and makes a realistic
discussion possible.

The basic concept which we owe to Plowden is that of the
Educational Priority Area (EPA), an area in which the coexist-
ence of deprivations, slum housing, widespread poverty,
unskilled employment or actual unemployment, is sufficiently
marked to justify remedial expenditure on the school network
in order, in part, to compensate for the manifest deficiencies of
social life in its raw state.

Were such areas to be determined it would be perfectly possible, within the spirit of the recommendations of the Plowden Council, to undertake a serious programme of compensatory educational expenditure. Existing schools could be physically improved or replaced, before it is practicable to rehouse whole districts. More and better staff could be recruited and encouraged to remain in such districts. Staff could be trained to appreciate some of the problems of deprivation and even to elaborate a pedagogy of deprivation. The concept of a 'neighbourhood teacher' could become meaningful. The teaching aids best suited to awaken the intelligence and curiosity of slum children could begin to be elaborated. More, the schools themselves could become, to a degree, centres of social regeneration: growth points of a new social consciousness among the poor, which might at last bring poverty under attack from its sufferers, no less than from the all-too-small battalions of liberal welfare workers and social administrators.

Obviously many of these are sensible aims. Yet it is important at the same time to state baldly what these aims could *not* achieve. Education, in itself, will not solve the problem of poverty. The social structure that generates poverty generates its own shabby education system to serve it; and while it is useful to attack the symptom, the disease itself will continually find new manifestations if it is not understood and remedied. The solution to poverty involves, of course, the redistribution of income, but more than that, it requires the redistribution of effective social power. Self-confidence, no less than material welfare, is a crucial lack of the poor, and both can only be won by effective joint action. More contentiously, it seems to us that educational provision alone cannot solve even the problem of educational poverty, if only because in this sphere there are *no* purely educational problems. The world of the poor is one in which it pays to keep your head down, in which the Good Soldier Schweik is more of a mentor than any of the great liberal heroes, and in which the motivations of liberal educationalists have never been very widely shared. Education in such an environment, if it is to succeed in encouraging people's full capabilities, must start out as training for community action, for self-help and mutual defence. More, poor people need to achieve self-respect *in spite* of the institutions that have kept them poor. They will never awaken to a cultural heritage acceptable to the majority of reformers simply in response to acts of administrative favour. This is not to say that such acts of favour should necessarily be rejected. In fact, they are all too few.

Limited though they were, the Plowden recommendations have, to date, fallen on barren ground. All have been diluted, and then applied hesitantly, sparingly and with more noise than effect.

Firstly there is the question, what constitutes an EPA? The definitional decisions on this matter obviously affect the value of any action which is taken within them.

Now although the Plowden Report was in fact ambiguous about the precise characteristics of an EPA, there was no doubt that what was intended was the designation of whole localities, distinct geographical districts, for priority treatment. Certainly EPAs are not to be equated with anything so random as existing school catchment areas. So far, however, this is precisely the equation that the Department of Education and Science has made.

The disadvantages of existing school catchment boundaries are plain to see. In our survey of the St Ann's district of Nottingham we showed that some 1·5 per cent of the children of the area gained places in grammar schools. The local Director of Education immediately produced figures to show that we were wrong and that the real figure was something like four times that total. It transpired that he was counting the number of grammar school places awarded to children attending primary schools which were situated within the geographical area of St Ann's. Naturally, the catchments of these schools ran over into adjacent, and it so happens, predominantly middle-class districts. The difference in the two figures can be entirely accounted for by this discrepancy which reinforces the view that middle-class children are greatly favoured and slum children greatly deprived inside the present structure. When the Nottingham Director was questioned on this matter, he told a reporter of the *Observer* that he was bound to collect statistics by schools, since there was no other workable definitional basis. But if there are to be Educational Priority *Areas*, it is quite obvious that the data about them must be made available for the Areas as such, if any sensible policy decisions are to ensue.

It is only fair to add that the LEA in Nottingham protested very strenuously, and with obvious justification, when the Department of Education and Science came to allocate the funds for incremental payments to teachers in 'Plowden Schools'. Two adjacent primary schools in the city had been designated as deserving these payments: one, an infant school, received them, while its neighbour, a junior school, did not. It is surely difficult to see how such a decision could be upheld within the terms of the Plowden Report.

By far the largest amount of money yet allocated to the 'Plowden Programme' was the sum of £16 million announced in the DES Circular 11/67 in August 1967. This sum was to be spent exclusively on school buildings, and LEAs were invited to submit to the Department proposals either for new buildings or for improvements to existing structures. It is, of course, true that the Circular stipulated that the schools nominated should be situated within districts suffering from 'the social or physical deficiencies which the Plowden Council had in mind'. These deficiencies are, however, outlined only very vaguely in the Plowden Report. Circular 11/67, far from giving some more coherent indication, made the Plowden list seem, by contrast, painfully precise, settling for the limp suggestions that 'a concentration of crowded, old, substandard and badly maintained houses is the most obvious and generally accepted sign of the sort of district the Plowden Council had in mind', and asserting that the Secretary of State 'does not intend to designate or define EPAs, from the centre in a formal way'.

The Circular became altogether more businesslike when it described the sort of detailed proposal which would attract the then Secretary of State's favour. He welcomed the replacement of old schools, or the improvement of existing ones, the construction or conversion of staff rooms, the extension of play space and the construction of facilities which would help to involve parents in the life of the school. Desirable, however, as each and all of these suggestions were, and badly needed as they still undoubtedly are, they were *not* the Plowden Programme. For practical and administrative convenience the key notion which informed the Plowden recommendation was apparently shelved, the educational priority *schools* have replaced EPAs. But the Department has not shelved with this notion the conventional wisdom that lay behind it. The final paragraph of the Circular proclaimed that

better educational provision can, by compensating for the effects of social deprivation and the depressing physical environment in which many children grow up, make an important contribution to overcoming family poverty. Better education is the key to improved employment opportunities for young people in these districts and to enabling them to cope with the social stresses of a rapidly changing society.

Perhaps, if there were to be a major social welfare programme in a specific area, even, maybe, hinged around the educational system, but also involving allied programmes of overall income-redistribution, community organization, together with policies of housing redevelopment and the encouragement of grass-roots participatory groupings at all levels of social activity, then, again perhaps, it is just remotely conceivable that family poverty could be brought under attack, by creating institutions in which poor people might begin to gain sufficient self-confidence to overcome some of the effects of social deprivation. What is not conceivable at all is that these desirable results will flow from the division of £16 million among 150 schools in fifty-one LEAs, even if this amount were only the first of a hundred such sums.

The notion of the priority area has, for all this, a positive significance precisely because it breaks through the arbitrary boundaries of a sectional administration and enables the problems of deprivation to be discussed as a whole. In its light, one may see, however feebly, a little more clearly the limitations of the present fragmented social welfare policies; equally one might begin to apprehend the possibilities for an integrated and imaginative social intervention. With Circular 11/67 even this small measure of light was extinguished.

What results should we expect of this modest and unimaginative effort? Most of the resources have been spent on necessary, but essentially minor, building improvements to a small number of the very worst schools in our decaying slums. Adding on an additional classroom here, and replacing a lavatory-block there, is, of course, worthy work, which will make a slight but genuine improvement to the handful of schools concerned. But even at the level of physical planning alone, this is in no sense a public committment to match the scale and gravity of the problem of antiquated school buildings. Needless to say, it represents no progress at all in the equally vital areas of teacher-recruitment and training, teaching methods and aids, or the other, less tangible aspects of educational deprivation.

At the same time, all is not lost. The Department of Education and Science and the Social Science Research Council are jointly sponsoring an EPA Action Research programme, at a total cost of £175,000. Five projects have been started in five different towns and cities, which go further than tinkering with the physical fabric of the schools. These projects include quite dramatic experiments in teaching methods and curriculum, and they endeavour to involve the local community and the parents of the pupils in the educational process. It is still too soon for a considered assessment of these particular schemes, although the indications are that the problems of multiple deprivation are proving more intractable than the most optimistic experimenters anticipated. In due course the final reports on these schemes will provide us with a detailed account of the difficulties encountered and the progress made, which will help to outline the effective limits of this approach to social improvement.

A few other recent developments hold out some promise. In the spring of 1969, the Home Office responded to the Gulbenkian Report on *Community Work and Social Change* (1968) by announcing a limited community development programme which would be concerned with 'the total personal needs of families and the community as a whole – an attempt to bridge the gap between the street and the offices of the various departments of welfare.' This scheme, which, like the EPA Action Research programme, is so far confined to a handful of localities, does demonstrate a willingness, in some quarters, to break away from traditional institutional and bureaucratic frameworks. Similarly the Urban Aid programme, involving as it does the Home Office, and the education, housing and welfare departments, represents a slight shift away from the conventional, departmental approach to social policy.

But these are all modest schemes, and only the most modest results can be expected of them. None the less they are items on the credit side of the ledger, and we must take what comfort we can from them. For the last five years has, on balance, been a period of further social and economic deterioration for the poor and underprivileged; a deterioration which has in the last two years intensified quite catastrophically, as it altered from being an unintended consequence of the hapless Labour Government's policies to become a deliberate and specific policy of the present administration.

The continuing decline of the economy, and the constantly rising unemployment statistics have greatly increased the abiding insecurity of the poor and economically vulnerable. Successive governments have been unable or unwilling to confront the structural obstacles to social advancement. But the present Government has deliberately, and as a matter of considered policy, determined to add to the burdens of the poor. In this policy, Mrs Thatcher has been able to play a conspicuous part. The slashing of the school-meals service, and the abolition of free school milk (a measure of such squalid meanness that the Secretary of State has been obliged to introduce an Act of Parliament to impose her will upon reluctant local authorities) has already eroded the fragile living standards of poor children everywhere. Accounts from one LEA after another reveal that the numbers of children taking school-dinners has dropped, in some cases by as much as a third. In the last few months reports from school medical officers announce the reappearance among some of their charges of the deficiency diseases that mutilated so many children in the 1930s. One of the bitter lessons that has to be relearned by the children of the poor is how to stand on your own rickets.

Against this sombre background, it seems hardly likely that we can look to the present Government for the will to initiate the ambitious, broadly conceived and expensive programmes of social reconstruction necessary to confront the growing poverty and deprivation in our educational system.

# Lewis Owen and Colin Stoneman
## Education and the Nature of Intelligence

Lewis Owen, the son of a coalminer, taught for two
years at a grammar school, and was then head of
department in a Sheffield secondary school for five
years. Since then he has been a lecturer in the
Lady Mabel College of Education, near Sheffield.
Colin Stoneman has been lecturer in chemistry at the
University of Hull since 1964. He is on the editorial
board of the 'Spokesman'.

In 1969 Professor Arthur Jensen published a long article in the
*Harvard Educational Review* called 'How Much Can We Boost
IQ and Scholastic Achievement?' In essence this article spelt
out the view that individual differences in 'intelligence' are to a
major extent genetically determined, and also that some racial
and social classes are genetically inferior to others in intellectual
ability. This position immediately stirred up a violent controversy in American academic circles because of the way in which,
whether he liked it or not, what should have been presented as
tentative statements or hypotheses on Jensen's part were usable
by the popular press and reactionaries to bolster up racialist
positions and conservative social policies. Jensen defended himself against the social criticism by pointing out the qualifications
he had hedged round some of his assertions, but was incapable
of answering the charges of unjustifiable generalization from
slight (and often ambiguous) evidence.

Now the debate, with all its unsavoury characteristics, and
unjustified appeals to 'science' and 'objectivity' has spread to
this country with the recent publication of *Race, Intelligence and
Education* by Professor H. J. Eysenck. This book is basically a defence of Jensen, but also elaborates the similar views that Eysenck
has himself held for some time. The purpose of this article

is not so much to criticize these views point by point as to look at the whole context of the controversy, and to try to make it comprehensible to non-psychologists. We shall be concerned with the nature of intelligence, its relation to I Q, the extent to which both are influenced by genetic, environmental and other factors, and the genetic basis of heritability.

In criticizing the views of Jensen and Eysenck we are not adopting an 'environmentalist' position, in the sense of wanting to deny the importance of genetic constitution. Rather we are concerned to emphasize that the nature of intelligence is exceedingly complex, that any single measure of it conceals more than it discloses, and that even specific factors of intelligence are determined by a complex interaction between genetic and environmental factors.

## The nature of intelligence

Perhaps the most familiar theory of intelligence, but, it should be emphasized, only one of several, has as its leading exponents the late Professor Sir Cyril Burt and Professor P. E. Vernon. This is the theory adopted by Jensen and Eysenck, but rejected by an increasing number of modern psychologists. Essentially the approach derives from Charles Spearman's belief in a single universal factor of intelligence, $g$, at the top of a hierarchy above a number of less important but more specific group factors such as verbal ability, numerical ability and so on. Although they concede a small part (about one fifth) to the effects of environment, this general intelligence factor is largely determined, they maintain, by heredity. It is important to realize that they lay stress on Spearman's definition of $g$ as 'the ability to educe relations and correlates'; in Jensen's words 'these are essentially the processes of abstraction and conceptualization'. They claim that $g$ is the common factor in all tests of complex problem solving, and that when the term 'intelligence' is used in a psychological context it should be understood to be referring to $g$.

A very different view of intelligence is described by Professor J. P. Guilford, who, in *The Nature of Human Intelligence* (1967) summarizes the evidence from many intelligence tests by himself and a number of other researchers that completely contradict the hierarchical view, the proponents of which have to date found it convenient to ignore his arguments almost completely. Guilford's book is very comprehensive, laying stress on the latest findings in genetics, neurology and the biological sciences. As he says:

Unfortunately, the most telling evidence against a universal factor in tests of intellectual performance is the decisive number of zero correlations that have been found when tests have been sufficiently varied in kind and have been constructed with good experimental control and when other experimental controls have been exercised in testing operations.

Guilford's own approach is summarized in an article in *New Education* (September 1965):

The multiple-factor view, which seems to be making substantial headway at present, assumes that, on the contrary, there are numerous unique intellectual abilities (but not an enormously large number) that collectively can be regarded as composing intelligence.... And with respect to the nature–nurture issue, there are, moreover, some indications that learning may well make substantial contributions to those abilities.

His theory, which he calls the 'Structure of Intellect' (S I) model, is complex, predicting 120 distinct factors of intelligence, of which over a hundred have been identified to date. Each factor has three aspects, or dimensions: Content, Operation and Product. 'Content' divides mental tasks into four categories: *figural*, concerned with concrete material of the kind perceived directly by the senses; *symbolic*, concerned with letters, numbers and so on; *semantic*, concerned with verbal meanings and ideas; and *behavioural* content, covering the general area of 'social intelligence'. 'Operation' specifies five ways of treating mental information: cognition, memory, evaluation, convergent production (or deducing one correct answer from given information, and divergent production (or thinking outwards to generate several possible answers or ideas). Finally each of the twenty ways of combining 'content' and 'operation' – for example the semantic-cognition factors – may operate on six different forms of 'product': units, classes, relations, systems, transformations and implications. Many of the resulting 120 factors are explained and demonstrated in *The Nature of Human Intelligence*, and a brief but quite detailed exposition is to be found in *Intelligence and Ability* edited by Stephen Wiseman (1967). Apart from the systematization of this model, and the possibility of demonstrating zero correlations between the factors, some categories are taken explicit notice of for the first time. Thus in *operation*, traditional intelligence tests rarely include divergent operation, which is closely connected with creativity. In *content*, behavioural abilities are often neglected.

Unlike Jensen and Eysenck, Guilford is open enough to summarize and examine theories contradictory to his own, but in so doing his model throws some light on the narrowness of the hierarchical theorists. 'If eduction of relations and correlates taken together are accepted as the *sine qua non* of *g*, then *g* embraces only eight of 120 intellectual abilities represented in the SI model.' His analysis of the then most recent revision of the Stanford–Binet tests suggested that among the 140 single tests, only twenty-eight of the intellectual factors of the SI theory were represented as compared with about eighty that had been identified at the time.

In flat contradiction to Eysenck's ill-informed and arrogant assertion that

the empirical data strongly support, and nowhere refute, the notion that our problem-solving behaviour in a great variety of different situations can be accounted for, as far as individual differences are concerned, by reference to a concept of general intelligence which is reasonably well measured by traditional intelligence tests.

Guilford explains how he was helped towards a rejection of the hierarchical approach by the fact that in a number of cases of factor analysis of intellectual tests in the United States: 'Almost no one reported finding a *g* factor; in fact, the tendency has been for each factor to be limited to a small number of tests in any analysis.' Nevertheless, Guilford does not treat his theory rigidly. The danger of any psychometric testing is that it may attempt to force people into predetermined categories, or to delimit possible abilities.

The structure of intellect as I have presented it to you may or may not stand the test of time. Even if the general form persists, there are likely to be some modifications. Possibly some different kind of model will be invented. Be that as it may, the fact of a multiplicity of intellectual abilities seems well established (Guilford's article in *Intelligence and Ability*.

The abandonment of hierarchical ideas, and with them the sub-servience of education to the concept of I Q, is a step that has indeed now been taken by a number of psychologists and educationists.

## Genes and heritability

The present state of genetics is not sufficiently advanced to allow any final choice to be made between the various theories of intelligence on this basis. However, some of the evidence it provides is more easily explicable in terms of the SI model than hierarchical models with an all-important $g$ factor measured by I Q. If we investigate certain attributes of a group of individuals, for example their height or measured I Q, it is often found that the attribute follows an approximately 'normal' distribution in the population. That is, most individuals are near to average height or I Q, and the further we go away from the mean, the fewer individuals we find: few men are over six feet tall or under five feet, fewer still are over seven feet or under four feet. This is just what we would expect to find in a population for an attribute the variation of which is due to a number of causes each of small effect. This is true whether these causes are genetic or environmental, or a combination of the two. It is generally accepted that the major cause in the case of height is genetic, and that a number of gene pairs is involved, all contributing small negative or positive increments to the height (for a more precise illustration of the process, see C. O. Carter, *Human Heredity*, 1970). There is also substantial evidence that genetic factors are important in the determination of I Q as commonly defined, and Jensen and Eysenck are concerned to emphasize the high heritability of I Q, which they estimate at about 80 per cent, leaving only 20 per cent for non-genetic factors. The importance of such factors is discussed in the next section.

What needs to be discussed at this stage is the relevance of heritability estimates for complex attributes like intelligence. Jensen and Eysenck of course play down the complexity, not least in their allegiance to $g$, and in implicit analogies with height. They consider that a large number of gene pairs contribute to the determination of $g$, and that the majority of these are directly concerned with its determination, though often by way of more specific lower order factors. They do not, however, consider the implications of the possibility that these factors (and many more involved in the SI model) are independent of each other. Guilford's test evidence for this has been mentioned above, and we will turn to the genetic evidence shortly. But it should be recognized that even if there is no physical or intellectual justification for combining a number of independent factors, it can still be done mathematically, and that if each of the component factors is distributed normally, then the (meaningless) combination of these factors will be distributed normally as well. Consider for example an illegitimate combination of height (reduced to a height quotient) and a count of ridges seen in fingerprints (similarly adapted). As both these attributes are roughly normally distributed, we could work out a combined quotient, even though the two are not correlated, and hopefully call it a 'physical quotient' (PQ) or some such thing. Two mistakes could then easily follow: firstly to assume that because an individual was above average in his PQ, his height must be above average; secondly to assume that the PQ tells us something about other physical characteristics (such as waist measurement or muscular strength) which had not been included in its calculation (some *indication* would be given if the characteristic were correlated with PQ). The analogy with IQ will be obvious, pointing the dangers of reliance on IQ, or concern with its heritability, if in fact some of its component factors are independent of each other (*a fortiori* if they are negatively correlated), or if important constituents of intelligence have been omitted, or underweighted.

The above discussion will have indicated that genetics does not work with a single subject, whose development is studied, but with populations of individuals. Now at the lowest estimates there are over seventy million million potential human genotypes, (or distinguishable combinations of genetic make-up). However, we cannot directly observe any genotype, but only the phenotype (or actual outcome of development of the genotype, which may be defined to include not only physical but also intellectual, emotional and cultural characteristics). Each genotype therefore has the potential to develop into a whole range of possible phenotypes. But this range, which is dependent on every aspect of the environment as well as on the nature of the genotype itself, cannot be predicted in advance. All that can be done is to measure the occurrence of a certain attribute in a population *after* the attribute has developed (or at best in intermediate stages of its development). In other words a heritability statement can refer only to a specific population, in a specific environment, and furthermore at a specific time (for gene frequencies change from one generation to the next). In the words of Sir Ronald Fisher, a heritability coefficient is 'one of those unfortunate short-cuts which have emerged in biometry for lack of a more thorough analysis of the data'. In the study of man, heritability statements turn out to be unreliable and deceptive.

The vast number of possible human genotypes arises from the fact that man possesses something like one hundred thousand genes. Although these are arranged in twenty-three pairs of chromosomes, the integrity of the latter are not preserved over generations because of exchanges of genes. Professor J. Hirsch estimates that 'there may be as many as 400,000 comparisons to be made between any two populations or races' (see his article in the *Bulletin of the Cambridge Society for Social Responsibility in Science*, July 1970, special issue, which we have drawn on to a large extent in writing this section). He continues

we know enough to expect no two populations to be the same with respect to most or all of the constituents of their gene pools. Mutations and recombinations will occur at different places, at different times and with differing frequencies. Furthermore, selection pressures will also vary. So the number and kinds of differences between populations now waiting to be revealed in 'the more thorough analysis' recommended by Fisher literally staggers the imagination. It does not suggest a linear hierarchy of inferior and superior race.

We cannot make meaningful statements about heritability for any single individual; every individual has a unique genotype (ignoring identical twins), and its 'norm of reaction' (range of possible development) is unknown. Taken together this means that

no general statement . . . can be made about the assignment of fixed proportions to the contributions of heredity and environment either to the development of a single individual, because we have not even begun to assess his norm of reaction, or to the differences that might be measured among members of a population, because we have hardly begun to assess the range of environmental conditions under which its constituent members might develop.

It follows that to ask whether heredity or environment is more important in determining intelligence is to ask a pseudo-question. Further, we cannot assume, as Jensen and Eysenck do that if a heritability estimate is high, little room is left for improvement by environmental modification. 'High or low heritability tells us absolutely nothing about how a given individual might have developed under conditions different from those in which he actually did develop.' It can be of little significance if (for example) black Americans do less well than white Americans on one particular comparison, in one particular environment (assuming this can be arranged!). There are perhaps many thousands of other comparisons that could be made, following developments in an infinite number of other environments. Who can say that the blacks would not perform better than the whites in many of these hypothetical cases?

## Environment

We have reached the conclusion that 'nature or nurture?' is a pseudo-question. It is also clear that Jensen and Eysenck have demonstrated very little, even after a long process of attempting to 'eliminate environmental factors'. The methods they employed in attempting such an elimination have been very widely criticized. The heavy reliance on twin studies has been attacked by Professor D. H. Stott in the *British Journal of Psychology* (November 1966), and more recently in various articles by Professor Liam Hudson. They have too easily equated environment with socio-economic status. They have too briefly considered perinatal and motivational factors and judged that they cannot account for the observed difference in performance in I Q tests between black and white Americans. Let us therefore look at such factors, not with the intention of reinstating them as explanations of apparent inferiority, for the preceding section should have made such a task unnecessary, but because they are important constituents of any environment. If we accept that 'intelligence' is the result of a complex interaction between genetic constitution and environment, it becomes recognizable that we are not simply faced with a question of improving the environment, but also one of not accidentally worsening it. For example, it seems probable that many working-class children in this country are successively thrown into an inappropriate middle-class school environment (inappropriate in that by the age of five their phenotype is sufficiently different from that of middle-class children, even if there were no significant genotypic difference at conception), that they are then tested and usually found wanting by inappropriate tests (and not only IQ tests these days), and then relegated to an inferior school, or low stream where the environment 'recognizing their limitations' may be the reverse of what is needed to allow the full development of their potentialities. A recognition of how an environment is deficient or inappropriate is necessary before one can start to improve it.

Jensen recognizes that environment should be understood to include pre-natal conditions and nutrition in early life. As Professor P. E. Vernon puts it:

Apparently the infant brain is particularly vulnerable to dietary deficiencies during later pregnancy and early feeding, say from three months before to six months after birth. The damage occurring then to the brain cells from lack of protein, proper vitamins and other crucial elements may be irreversible; it cannot be made up even if the older infant or child is relatively well fed (*Intelligence and Cultural Environment*, 1969).

As Dr John Dobbing made clear at the meeting of the British Association for the Advancement of Science at Exeter in 1969, although this is primarily a problem of great importance to the underdeveloped countries, there are also sections of the community in Britain today whose babies are at risk. (See also his article in *Science Journal*, May 1967.)

There is further support for this in an article by Professor S. P. R. Rose in the *Cambridge Society for Social Responsibility in Science Bulletin* (1970), in which he explains how environmental deprivation can be less extreme than this and yet still stunt and retard the growth of intelligence. Experiments reveal how significant differences in brain enzyme content occur among animals reared in circumstances that are mentally stimulating.

Brain structure is affected by even quite brief exposure to novel or 'learning' situations. Under these circumstances changes in the rates of production of certain key bio-chemical substances within the brain (e.g. RNA and protein) can be shown to occur. Concurrently changes in the degree of connectivity of the brain cells takes place.

Rose also lays stress on sympathetic handling of the creatures concerned. Perhaps this can be extrapolated to human beings. Eric Berne in *Games People Play* (1964), describes how inadequate handling in infancy and inadequate attention and recognition cause the mental processes to atrophy. D. F. Mahon in an article in *English in Education* (1970) stresses the importance of handling and reciprocal attention between mother and child in the growth of intelligence. The growth of meaning and the enlargement of vocabulary in early infancy depend even more on the vocal–auditory loop between mother and child than on the child's cultural background. Moreover, a point that supports Rose's statements about animals brought up in environments differing in their cultural richness, when babies are raised in circumstances without stimulation, communication or vocalization, they are not developed at school entrance in manipulative skills or the use of language, and are thus at a serious disadvantage.

The search for 'culture-fair' tests is doomed to failure, even in the opinion of Professor P. E. Vernon, who has long been associated with a hierarchical view of intelligence:

We must give up the notion of intelligence as some mysterious power or faculty of the mind which everyone, regardless of race or culture, possesses in varying amounts and which determines his potentiality for achievement. In particular we must relinquish the will-o'-the-wisp that by avoiding verbal tests of intelligence and resorting to tests based on abstract materials like Progressive Matrices or performance tests, we can eliminate cultural handicaps and so arrive at a true measure of potential. There is no such thing as a culture-fair test, and never can be (*Bulletin of the British Psychological Society*, 1968).

And in *Intelligence and Cultural Environment* (1969) he writes:

We are not entitled to say that hereditary factors produce particular characteristics. ... What we can say is that man's capacities are not determined by his internal structure to the same extent as those of species lower in the evolutionary scale; they are built up in him to a greater extent through stimulation and learning. ... Admittedly, though, we have been too apt in the past to stress hereditary limitations.

The search for 'culture-fair' tests is doomed to failure because, no matter how far the tests attempt to isolate 'intelligence' by getting away from overt language structures (so obviously deeply influenced by environmental factors) and attempting to measure things such as non-verbal concept formation, one is still not escaping the influence of language to any significant extent. Professor M. M. Lewis in *Language, Thought and Personality in Children* (1963) has explained how, without the intervention of a language constantly practised and sharpened, it is extremely difficult for young children even to *perceive* objects properly. In an article in the *British Journal of Educational Psychology* in November 1968, E. Stones and J. R. Heslop found support for the argument that concepts are formed not merely through the interplay of associations but

through an intellectual operation in which all the elementary mental functions participate in specific combination. This operation is guided by the use of words as the means of actively centring attention, of abstracting certain traits, synthesising them and symbolizing them by a sign.

What is more, their tests showed a close association between the level of sophistication of concept-forming (dependent on language) and the ability to transfer such concepts to other situations. At the most primitive level in human beings, language enters into our mental processes, and few would argue that, in terms of the way our culture operates, working-class children are at a disadvantage when acquiring the kind of vocabulary and language structure that make classifying or concept-forming possible.

This does *not* mean, as Bernstein points out (on p. 113) that their language structures and habits are necessarily of inferior value to those of middle-class children. It means essentially that their use of language is of the type not conducive to success in that narrow band of abilities measured by IQ tests.

**Race, class and education**

Jensen and Eysenck believe that black Americans are inferior intellectually to whites. They believe that the Irish are similarly inferior to the English, and the British working-class to the middle class. We, along with many educational psychologists believe that the comparisons they have made are to a large extent arbitrary and their results of very limited significance. The data they have used have also been severely criticized from positions much closer to their own than ours is. Perhaps the most notable examples of this is in the results of two independent investigations recently completed in the United States. Jane Mercer used intelligence tests with black and Mexican Americans, and after careful matching of environment claimed to find a match in I Q scores with those of whites. Even those who were disadvantaged and scored low on the tests 'were very intelligent in their behaviour in the community'. George W. Mayeske studied achievement tests of over 100,000 students from all over America, and concluded that minority group children had suffered so much cultural deprivation by the time they reached school that no amount of education could bring them up to par. 'The differences among the racial–ethnic groups approach zero as more and more considerations related to differences in their social conditions are taken into account' (see the *Guardian*, 7 September 1971).

Theoretical and practical considerations therefore do not support abandonment of programmes designed to improve the education of the disadvantaged. To be fair to Jensen, although he considers that 'Compensatory education has been tried and it apparently has failed [despite] unprecedented support from Federal funds,' he has also categorically stated that he wants 'increased emphasis on these efforts, in the spirit of experimentation.' In Eysenck's hands this becomes: 'when the evidence from American studies is as clearly negative as seems to be the case, then only political prejudice outweighing all contrary evidence can persist in calling for expenditure of large sums of money on what must at present be regarded as a lost cause' (*Black Paper Two*). And it reaches its nadir with Kingsley Amis: 'intelligence is mainly an inherited characteristic and not much can be done to modify it by education or other means' (*Black Paper One*).

Our view could hardly be more different. In terms of Guilford's theory, it is not even necessary to postulate any environmental influence to get a profoundly different perspective. Suppose that only four of his 120 factors turn out to be completely independent, of significance intellectually, and determined independently of each other genetically (this is deliberately taking a very cautious view), then ignoring all other effects, it would follow that only one person in sixteen, or less than 7 per cent, would be below average in all of these abilities; or put another way, over 93 per cent of people would be *above* average in one or more of the abilities. With more independent factors, more people would excel in at least a few things. Although they might lack the particular combination of factors to perform certain intellectual tasks well, they would almost certainly have potentiality in other directions. This is a very different perspective from the present outlook which treats about 80 per cent of our children as if they are unlikely ever to excel at anything of any importance.

It remains to be asked whether we can begin to realize the implications behind these new ideas by bringing about the appropriate changes within the system we now have. The answer is that we can, at least in part. Nor is the process necessarily expensive. It depends primarily on the attitudes of teachers and administrators within the system. There are examples already of schools where children, formerly considered second rate, have improved their performance beyond recognition. One of us was a teacher at Birley Secondary Modern School, Sheffield where the headmaster, R. A. Davies, pioneered non-streaming from 1954. Under the influence of new motivations, in an atmosphere that was socially therapeutic and intellectually exciting, pupils of relatively low IQ made enormous progress. In what was by this time in the history of the school a not untypical year, 1966, the fifth-formers leaving that summer after a normal five-year unstreamed course, obtained an average of 3·3 O-level passes (better than the C-streams of most grammar schools). There were twenty-five in the class from a school of 300; they were not selected in any way, the only criterion being their desire to stay on into the fifth form. (In fact there were three in the group who, in their first year had been remedial pupils having considerable difficulties with reading and writing. What is more, we had lost a number of our most able pupils who had gone out to work, under parental influence.)

About eight of these twenty-five were capable of taking degrees, though some of them chose not to. One has just graduated and is doing research in astrophysics at London University, two others are in their final year of honours degrees, another is doing a Diploma of Art and Design, and a fifth has just been accepted as a mature student to do a degree in economics. It is noteworthy that the highest IQ in the group, when measured at eleven years, was 108, compared with a normal lower limit for entry to grammar schools of 114. Even with those who left school at fifteen or sixteen, the intellectual impetus has been maintained. For example, one boy from a different year group, who failed to gain any O-levels at school and was considered rather weak and certainly lazy, had within four years of leaving school gained three distinctions at A-level, read politics at university, and is now working for a Master's degree. This interest in further and higher education is widespread in the former pupils of this school.

Apart from mere examination results, there were numerous other indications of great intellectual progress. Nearly all the staff of the school felt that they were on the threshold of much more significant advances. Nor was this a particularly well-qualified staff. At Birley School, the really critical breakthrough only came when a majority of the staff began, under the guidance of the headmaster, to believe in the capacity of children to develop open-endedly. E. J. Goodacre (in *School and Home*, 1970) and D. A. Pidgeon (in *Expectation and Pupil Performance*, 1970) both underline the importance of teachers' attitudes in determining pupils' abilities. There was dramatic support for this idea from an experiment in the United States in 1968. Children who had been selected at random were divided into two groups, and the teachers of the children in one of the groups were then told that special tests had indicated that they were expected to increase their IQ over the next year. A year later these children had IQ increases of between ten and twelve points greater than those in the other group. One child increased from eighty-eight to 128, another from sixty to ninety-seven, and few failed to improve significantly (see *Pygmalion in the Classroom* by R. Rosenthal and L. F. Jacobson, 1968).

Most teachers, however, still tend to accept, often uncritically, the notion of fixed ability and the necessity for streaming; if they teach in secondary modern schools or low streams, they have probably come through the binary system as 'second-class' college of education students, while their 'first-class' colleagues, the graduates, are likely to be teaching in grammar schools or higher streams, at a higher level of pay, so that the class nature of the different levels of education is reinforced. This is one of the reasons why simply substituting comprehensive schools for the tripartite system will never on its own bring about equality of opportunity.

Unfortunately, recent research findings and the resulting new theories of intelligence will take some time to percolate down to teachers, as well as to parents, administrators and even to educational psychologists. This is not surprising, as the ideas involved are fairly complex and still developing, and furthermore run counter to the traditional modes of thought which still dominate our educational system, and which Eysenck hopes to preserve.

As Vernon says in *Intelligence and Cultural Environment*: 'Man has by no means reached the limits of his capacities – either of his own reasoning or of the tools he produces to work for him.' To realize this potential we need to make available to all our pupils, and incidentally to ourselves in the process, the potential riches latent in our schools and our society, through the adoption of non-streaming in a properly comprehensive system, through less formal curricula and teaching methods, where the emphasis is on the opportunities for children to explore and find out where their interests and abilities lie. But above all, we need more humble and hopeful attitudes on the part of teachers and administrators.

The approach we are recommending has already been undertaken by a number of junior and middle schools that we have visited: schools like Oyster Park Middle School, Castleford. They have begun to achieve truly astonishing results with working-class children – astonishing, that is, if you believe in the orthodox theory of fixed, inherited intelligence.

# David Rubinstein
# The Public Schools

**David Rubinstein taught history in London comprehensive schools from 1956 to 1965. Since 1965 he has been lecturer in social history at the University of Hull. He is the author of 'School Attendance in London, 1870-1904' (1969), co-author with Brian Simon of 'The Evolution of the Comprehensive School, 1926-1966' (1969) and has written other works on educational and recreational subjects.**

In considering the need to transform our education system we must not forget the existence of a sector of privileged schools. To take a small group of the wealthy and to educate them separately from the remainder of society is to assure the continuation of a class-ridden society such as contemporary England.

The First Report of the Public Schools Commission, published in 1968, is not a clarion call for the abolition of private education. In some respects it can be looked on as a whitewashing job. But it provides the factual basis for a devastating attack on the public schools and in certain statements it lays bare the worst features of those schools. While some of their more pernicious traits are now allegedly disappearing, the public schools remain fundamentally middle-class institutions; or perhaps more accurately, institutions engaged in educating the upper middle class in the traditional values of the ruling class. Moreover, 'those who can afford to opt out of the maintained system care less about its development'. These include politicians, administrators (such as the administrators of the state schools) and some of the Public Schools Commission's own members. 'If all influential parents had children in maintained schools, they would have brought pressure to bear on Parliament and Whitehall to make them better than they are.'

It might be thought that a mere recitation of the facts of inequality would induce a desire to do something about them.

In any case, the facts are instructive. In January 1967, 5·5 per cent of children attended independent schools, a drop from 9 per cent in 1947, and by 1969 the figure had further dropped to just under 5 per cent. The 273 public schools in England and Wales, those elite schools belonging to three associations of headmasters and headmistresses, contained 92,272 pupils of secondary age, under half of the children attending independent secondary schools and only 2·9 per cent of our secondary-school children. Yet these 92,272 pupils, and in particular the 39,674 boys boarding at public schools, have a tremendous influence over our whole education system.

The First Report of the Public Schools Commission shows that products of the 273 public schools mentioned above dominate the important positions in business, the law and the professions as they did when Tawney wrote *Equality* in the 1920s and as they did in the late nineteenth century. Consider the figures in the table.

It is of course true that these prominent men were at school many years ago, but there is no reason to suppose that the trend has altered. In the administrative class of the Civil Service, for example, the percentage of successful candidates who attended public schools actually increased between 1936 and 1967. This situation is reinforced by the fact that boys from public and other independent schools have the edge on entrance to Oxford and Cambridge. In 1965–6, 45 per cent of the closed awards for entry to Oxford went to boys from independent boarding schools. As the Robbins Report showed, public-school boys need lower qualifications to enter Oxford and Cambridge than do boys from other schools. Steven Watson, tutor at Christ Church, Oxford, wrote in December 1960:

The need to civilize those who are born to great responsibilities, the desire to be tender to the claims of loyal old members will, for a long time to come, continue to work to the benefit of the public schools rather than the obscurer grammar schools (quoted in H. Glennerster and R. Pryke, *The Public Schools*, 1964).

It would be a rash man who would say that the old-boy network no longer retains its strong meshes.

It is not, in short, the quality of their education alone which first sends the products of the public schools to Oxford and Cambridge and then enables them to become prominent in the upper reaches of Government, business and the professions. This owes even more to the fact that they come from a socio-economic elite and that their public-school background gives them easy entry into a select world.

| Category | Date | Percentage (whose school is known) who attend(ed) public schools |
|---|---|---|
| Fourteen year olds at school in England and Wales | 1967 | 2·6 |
| Seventeen year olds at school in England and Wales | 1967 | 9·3 |
| School leavers (England and Wales) going to all universities | 1965–6 | 15·6 |
| School leavers (England and Wales) going to Oxford and Cambridge | 1965–6 | 35·1 |
| Vice-chancellors, heads of colleges, professors at English and Welsh universities | 1967 | 32·5 |
| Heads of colleges, professors at Oxford and Cambridge | 1967 | 49·3 |
| Labour Cabinet | 1967 | 42·0 |
| Conservative Cabinet | 1963 | 90·9 |
| Labour MPs | 1966 | 19·5 |
| Conservative MPs | 1966 | 76·6 |
| Admirals, generals, air marshals | 1967 | 55·0 |
| Physicians and surgeons at London teaching hospitals and on General Medical Council | 1967 | 68·0 |
| Directors of prominent firms | 1967 | 70·8 |
| Church of England Bishops | 1967 | 75·0 |
| Judges and QCs | 1967 | 79·2 |
| Fellows of Royal Society elected | 1962–6 | 24·6 |
| Governors and directors of the Bank of England | 1967 | 76·5 |

Source: Public Schools Commission, First Report, vol. II, 1968, p. 236.

It goes almost without saying that the public schools are privileged in terms of staff, equipment and facilities. Whereas the London County Council aimed after the Second World War to provide schools of three and a half acres for up to 1000 pupils in Inner London (and did not always achieve this ratio), many public schools have half an acre or more *for each child*. Stowe School has 600 boys and 750 acres. In 1967 about 100 independent schools had a teacher–pupil ratio more generous than 1:7·5. In 1970 (no later figures are available) the ratio in primary independent schools recognized by the Department of Education and Science as efficient was 1:13·1; in independent secondary schools, 1:11·0. This compares with the 1970 figures for council schools – 1:27·4 in primary schools, 1:18·8 in secondary moderns, 1:17·4 in comprehensives and 1:16·4 in grammar schools.

Of course all this has to be paid for, and in an inflationary age there seems to be no difficulty in finding the money. I give below the fees for 1971 for boarding pupils at three leading boys' and three girls' public schools, with the fees for 1969, the date when this article was first written, in brackets: Eton £765 (£684), Harrow £759 (£669), Winchester £765 (£672), Benenden £750 (£645), Cheltenham Ladies' £606 (£558), Roedean £732 (£651). It would be easy to find similar (if somewhat lower) figures for other schools, and it is clear that most fees have risen sharply since 1967, when the Public Schools Commission found that the average annual fee for boarding pupils at public schools was £510 for boys, £454 for girls. It is no wonder that the schools are filled almost exclusively from a tiny proportion at the top of the social pyramid. A revealing if unguarded remark made by George Snow, former headmaster of Ardingley, shows just how remote the public-school atmosphere is from real life. 'All society,' Snow claimed in a book published in 1959, 'from the duke's son to the shopkeeper's boy, is found there. Only the wage earner is normally excluded.' This privileged state of things, moreover, is heavily subsidized by the taxpayer, as the Commission's researches show. In 1965–6 nearly £9 million, over 10 per cent of the income of the recognized independent (including public) schools, was provided by central or local governments. Rate relief, exemption from Selective Employment Tax and relief on covenants to schools amounted to well over £4 million. Finally, favourable tax regulations enable school fees to be paid by covenants to grandchildren, by endowment assurance, and other methods of reducing tax liability. One loophole was closed by the 1968 Finance Act, under which children's unearned income was aggregated jointly with their parents' for tax purposes. But, saying: 'I am convinced that that legislation was misconceived,' the Conservative Chancellor of the Exchequer, in a piece of real Tory philosophy in practice, announced the ending of this restriction in his Budget speech in March 1971. Commenting on the change, the *Guardian* pointed out that it would be 'to the delight of the public schools', and added that the concession would be of no help to the poor. 'Working-class children do not have private incomes' (31 March 1971). Thus we have a situation in which the state gives both financial and moral support to the continuation of a system of education specifically designed to preserve social-class barriers.

Thus far the case may perhaps be considered as established. What we must now ask ourselves is whether we can hope to reform the public-school system without a social revolution. Are the public schools merely the tip of the iceberg of social inequality, not amenable to change without basic changes in our social structure?

Such questions miss the point. To leave the public schools alone until a social revolution occurs is to give up the struggle in the educational field. Public schools dominate British life in a way independent schools dominate the life of no other nation; their abolition would give an immense fillip to the state system.

It may be, as the Public Schools Commission asserts, that some of the more obnoxious features of public-school life are on the way out. According to the Commission corporal punishment and fagging are on the decline, the importance of games has been reduced and 'school spirit' is no longer the thought-controlling influence of the past. The Commission may be right, though a reading of such books as John Wakeford's *The Cloistered Élite* (1969) may leave some doubt on this point. In any case it is rare for these features of public-school life to have been abandoned completely. The public-school ethos remains powerful, along with the evils of single-sexed education and the un-questioning assumption that boarding school (starting at age eight in prep schools) is the right form of upbringing for our future rulers. Such an education not only leaves the desired mark on those who experience it, but in various ways influences most state secondary schools to try to inculcate similar values in their pupils. For example, the prefect system and the insistence on ridiculous caps perching on the heads of six-foot sixth formers in a 'good' comprehensive school can hardly be seen except as the apeing of the public-school tradition. And for an indication of the tenacity of that tradition we may note Wakeford's conclusion:

Over the last century the staff have exhibited a conspicious reluctance to change the basic structure of the schools or to attempt extensive experimentation with new organizational forms. Unlike a small number of their distinguished predecessors, the headmasters direct their energies more to defending present organizational structures than to changing them.

In 1964 Harold Wilson told the House of Commons that nobody in his Government had attended any of the schools which he had attended. This was certainly an improvement on 1945 when Clement Attlee deliberately chose as his Parliamentary Private Secretary a fellow Old Haileyburian. But such things are still far from uncommon, and as J. B. Priestley once wrote:

It is unnatural, rather sinister, for middle-aged men ... to be wondering and asking about one another's schools. .... A large section of English life, public as well as private, is strongly influenced by school-boy values (*New Statesman*, 20 July 1962).

Education for democracy means that those who are in greatest need should receive the greatest advantages. Our present system, on the contrary, ensures that children – and, in particular, boys – of the wealthiest parents receive a privileged education, an open door to the best universities and professions, as well as an education which remains barbaric in certain respects. An undue proportion of financial and human resources are devoted to a tiny, privileged sector of the school population, while at the same time practices entirely unsuited to a democratic age are perpetuated. Most of these children, as the Public Schools Commission observes, 'would have been away to a good start whatever school they went to'. Our values, in short, are the reverse of what they should be. Without absorbing the independent, and particularly the public schools, into the state system, any talk of education for democracy remains a mockery.

# Part Three
**Primary**

# David Sturgess
## Happenings in a Primary School

David Sturgess taught mathematics in schools for eight years and was head of a mathematics department in a college of education for six years. He is now lecturer and tutor-in-charge of the Mathematics Advisory Unit at the School of Education of Nottingham University. He has worked closely for a number of years with the staff of a primary school on developing new approaches to teaching. He is the author of several articles on the teaching of mathematics and the editor of 'Teaching Mathematics: Main Courses in Colleges of Education' (1967).

When I have been working with primary-school teachers in their classrooms, on several occasions I have been asked: 'Is what I am doing all right?' These same teachers are often surprised when I discuss with them work that I have seen and admired in their classrooms.

The surprise is because they are doing what they feel is obvious and are not aware that it does not happen in every classroom. The question about the success of what they are doing arises out of a deep concern that they shall do the very best for the children in their charge and not from a desire for praise.

These teachers are working on intuition with the backing of knowledge and in many cases a great deal of experience. They believe that the acquisition of knowledge as the only criterion for progress does not form a satisfactory basis for the education of children, and yet it is difficult to formulate in precise terms this broader concept of education, although its effects are apparent within many primary schools.

Many writers have criticized contemporary education on the grounds that phrases such as 'child-centered' cover a multitude of evils and some good. And yet what does one put in their place? One must ask what criteria are being used by a teacher in deciding whether he has been successful or not in his aims. The aim might be described as 'to enable a child to fulfil his potential', but how do we decide a child's potential or how do we know when it has been fulfilled?

I see a danger that the present IQ tests, verbal-reasoning tests, etc., will be replaced by another set of tests designed to test children's potential ability to cooperate or to contribute to group work; this could have as stultifying an effect upon the many remarkable things that are happening in classrooms all over the country as the eleven-plus has had in the past. We are crying 'out with the old orthodoxy' only to replace it with a new one.

I want to suggest a way of avoiding this, whilst at the same time stating our values more clearly than is stated in terms such as 'child-centered' or 'fulfilling potential'. All the teaching that I have experienced that has thrilled and excited me has been based on intuition and experience. I would not like to say how much of each for it probably varies with the situation, but I imagine the degree of intuition that comes into play is what marks out the exceptional teacher from the good one. If we wish therefore to find criteria to judge the success of work with children we must take into account these two important factors of the situation which seem to me impossible to measure. To do this we must first believe in their value. If a teacher asks: 'Am I doing the right thing?' the answer should be: 'What do you think? Does the children's achievement measure up to what you instinctively feel it should be?'

Unfortunately it is possible to delude ourselves rather easily about the nature of instinctive behaviour. It is much better if such judgements are the subject of discussion with others. One way in which this could be done is to treat the accounts given by other people of what they observe against our own experience in a similar situation. If I give an account of my observations and say what I value in this situation, I cannot ask others automatically to accept my values, but I can ask them to examine similar situations which they may have experienced to see if they value the same things.

As an example of the kind of thing that I have in mind, I offer the following accounts of personal experience. One took place in a junior school, the other in an infant school on the same campus. Neither school would probably be willing to accept the label 'progressive', but both head teachers run their schools in ways they would probably not have considered possible ten or fifteen years ago.

The junior school put on a concert for parents on two evenings. Nearly every child in the school contributed to this concert and items were given by forms, or combined forms, and by a choir which contained several age groups. The only individual items were some children speaking some short poems that they or other children had written. This must seem to be a description that would fit a similar activity in many junior schools – and yet I believe there were some important differences.

Most of the parents had arrived in good time before the concert began and were already beginning to find the seats rather small when the headmaster introduced the evening by asking us to 'join with' the children in their activities. And this is precisely what happened. One had the feeling, not of being in an audience, but of being involved with the children in what they were doing as if one had eavesdropped on a normal day-to-day occurrence. It is significant that many of the items were in fact ordinary classroom situations. There was an infectious enjoyment about everything that was done. Quite a long play performed in French was extremely amusing (intentionally) and had the audience spellbound in spite of the fact that many did not understand a word. A girl doing cartwheels in a dance got carried away and tried one too many – ending up in rather a giddy state on the floor. One of the children taking part in the country dancing never quite got in phase with the others at a particular moment. And yet – here was a motley collection of adults sitting on uncomfortable chairs in a very cramped situation for two hours without a cough or a shuffle or a mumbled conversation with their neighbour. Total involvement – why? It was a shared experience, there seemed to be a very real sense in which these children were not performing for the entertainment of the adults but inviting them to share an experience in which they themselves found pleasure.

It is difficult to say how this was achieved, but to an onlooker certain things were noticeable. One was the lack of inhibition on the part of the children – it did not matter if things went slightly wrong because they nearly always did and there were no teachers frowning at them or nagging them to do things. To anyone who did not know them it would have been impossible to tell which of the audience were staff and which were parents – and yet all this had not happened by magic. One of the things that must have communicated itself to the audience was the sense of trust developed between these children and their teachers that enabled them to sit back knowing that whatever happened the children would do their best and this was all that mattered. Part of the enjoyment that came across could well be a direct result of a complete lack of fuss or flap or regimentation.

It is also perhaps significant that when the children were not actually taking part they were not locked in a classroom with a teacher–jailer, but were either entertained or found their own entertainment on the school field, and yet were never visible. I afterwards learned that a teacher of some of the youngest children gathered them round her at 9 o'clock (the concert went on till 9.30) and quietly read them a story in one of the classrooms.

The infant school headmistress regularly invites parents to attend morning assembly at school, sometimes for special events like Harvest Thanksgiving, sometimes on an ordinary day. Always what takes place is the same as on a normal day. On this occasion some of the children were due to take part in a musical festival and the parents were invited in so that the children might have the opportunity of singing to an adult audience.

The parents arrived promptly at 9.15 a.m. and were occupying seats in rows at one side of the hall when one of the older children rang a bell. The welfare assistant put a record on the gramophone and in a leisurely way doors opened round the hall and children began to come in, not in twos or in 'crocodiles' but in all kinds of groupings. The headmistress moved to the front of the hall and sat on a chair facing the children with a book open in front of her. Still the children came in and as they came in they sat down – anywhere. Some children sat down with the friends they had come in with, some children looked for children from other classes and sat with them. Teachers came in bringing chairs with them and also quietly sat down. One or two children had difficulty in deciding where to sit and wandered round for some time before deciding on a place. At the end one boy was left standing and shuttled between two or three places trying to decide where to go until finally he sat down. When the last child had sat down there was a short pause and then with no other preliminaries the headmistress, still sitting on her chair, quietly read a prayer.

The whole proceeding seemed to be without tension of any sort. In spite of parents being present there was not the slightest sign of strain on the part of any of the teachers. No one said to the boy 'Do hurry up and sit down' and his face showed no strain. I felt that he was not in the least concerned that he was the last and that he could not make up his mind.

Why should he be if no one else was?

At the end of the assembly the children were asked to sing their songs. No pushing and shoving, just 'Get in two lines so that you can see me' from the headmistress, and there it was – accomplished. When they had finished, the whole school was invited to join in the last song (which they did with obvious enjoyment) and all but the choir were asked to return to their classes. This they did from all points of the hall; no pushing, rushing or shoving, not a single teacher said a word. The choir were then asked to sit down facing the parents and the parents invited to comment on their singing.

Many will claim that these two accounts are emotive and subjective pieces of writing that evaluate nothing. I agree that they are subjective and emotive, but would claim that they are in a certain sense 'evaluative'. One way of evaluating the present educational trends is by recording as simply as possible what *actually* happens and then saying what we value about these situations. How can one measure, in any sense at all, the value of the perception of an experienced teacher who knows the right moment to call a number of excited and tired young children together and read them a story?

The things I value here the freedom and respect shown to the children in these situations. Far too many school 'concerts'

are like watching performing animals at a circus. The children
are put through their paces for the approval or disapproval of
the parents. It is rare to be invited to share in the enjoyment of
doing what comes naturally, but at the same time this is putting
the children on a level with their audience. There are no per-
formers and audience but a corporate body of children and
adults joining together to enjoy themselves. I value the fact that
adult tensions were not imposed on this situation. The children
were allowed to be as relaxed as possible in these situations
and mistakes or difficulties in making decisions did not matter
because there was no one worrying about them – at least in
any obvious way. No doubt the teachers did experience tensions
but this never showed in actions or words.

There is nothing soft or wishy-washy about this kind of
freedom. The children who can walk into an assembly and sit
where they like and then walk out again at the age of six without
any formal organization are highly disciplined, but in a most
constructive way. They are being asked to exercise *self*-discipline
and then being *trusted* by the teacher to do this properly. Children do not behave in such an uninhibited yet disciplined way as
the junior children did without there being mutual trust between teacher and child, the kind of trust which in my own
education was exceedingly rare and which is significantly lacking
in the adult world in which we live.

None of this could have been achieved without hard work and
effort on the part of the teachers. As I said earlier, neither of
these head teachers would regard themselves as 'progressive'
because this has overtones of 'keeping up with the Joneses',
and what they are doing arises from deep convictions about their
responsibilities in the education of children. But I believe that
the experience that these children have in corporate living during
the five to six years they spend in these schools will profoundly
affect their attitudes to other people in adult life. It is important
to realize that the events described are most unlikely to happen
in isolation. Children behave in this way on the one occasion
because it is part of the everyday atmosphere in which they live
and work. The concert was merely an extension of things that
are happening every day in the classroom.

One consequence of this attitude is that these children are

highly critical, but in a constructive way, of the authoritarian behaviour of some teachers at the secondary level. One child, when asked how she liked her first week at secondary school, replied, 'It will be all right when someone tells us what to do, instead of keep telling us what not to do.'

I have tried to describe feelings, atmosphere, a sense of corporate behaviour. Unfortunately many people see these things but do not understand them. I believe that we should make an effort to explain to people not directly concerned with education (except as parents) those things which we value in contemporary education at its best. The difficulty that faces us is how to explain something that needs to be experienced in a sympathetic and receptive way for its full impact to be understood. I hope that what I have suggested in this essay will enable more people to understand what is, or could be, available to our children.

# John Mitchell
# Freedom in the Junior School

**John Mitchell has been deputy head and head of
Rusholme St Agnes's Church of England School,
Manchester, for the last eight years. With the increase
in the proportion of children of immigrants in the
school, standards began to fall, but they have since been
maintained by adopting individual approaches and
dropping the previous formal methods.**

Recently much criticism has been levelled at the methods which
have been introduced into infant- and junior-school teaching
over the last few years. There seems to be a growing body of
opinion which feels that the progressive primary school is little
more than a child-minding establishment where the children
are subject to no discipline and are given no directed teaching;
if in fact they learn anything at all, it is by way of a 'bonus' and
is purely accidental. As the head of a junior and infant school I
have become accustomed to Mother's 'Oh, yes, he seems very
happy at school. In fact he can't get there quickly enough, but
he tells us that all he does is play. When is he going to get down
to some serious work?' or 'She's been at school six weeks now
and she still hasn't been given a reading book. When are you
going to teach her the alphabet?' When I hear these questions
and others like them, I know that once again I must attempt to
justify modern approaches to learning. All adults have attended
school as children and so, to some extent, they can claim to have
some knowledge of what takes place, but of necessity the experience of junior schools of most parents is at least fifteen
years out of date. They remember the authoritarian approach
of their childhood and are puzzled when they discover that their
children are not taught in the same way. Their ignorance is understandable, but I find that if the aims and methods are ex-

plained and evidence of their success provided, parents will go away feeling satisfied that their child is being efficiently educated.

To the uninformed a walk round the modern primary school can be a confusing experience. No longer are the children rigidly marshalled in long silent lines threading their way through gloomy bare corridors. Nor will a glance through a classroom window reveal neat rows of desks occupied by silent listening (or did they just *appear* to be listening?) children – all eyes directed on the teacher. In the old type of school if the visit does not coincide with 'playtime' or lunch time one is likely to be aware only of the school's silence and of its lack of children. All the pupils will be tidily stowed away out of sight in their uniform boxes – forty or so children and one teacher in a room isolated from a number of similar groups who together make up the school. Few children will be seen in corridors and, unless it is being used for a music or physical education lesson, the school hall will be empty – a large area of valuable but wasted space.

If one visits a less formal school it is probable that the contrast will be most marked. The first impression will be that this building exists to be used by children; they will be seen everywhere. The corridors and hall will not stand empty, as classes overspill into them. The modern school sees little value in passive listening, but places great stress on active learning: not, as its critics say, playing, but directed learning through the child's interests and active participation.

The role of the primary school should be to give the children the belief that learning is a pleasure. We need to bring them to the stage where they want to learn because they recognize for themselves the value of knowledge; and then it is up to the teachers to channel this desire along suitable paths. Only an elementary knowledge of child development is necessary to be aware that all children are at different stages of intellectual, social and physical development, and they need to be treated as individuals, with special attention being paid to their own particular strengths and weaknesses. When taking a traditional lesson it is impossible to meet the individual demands of all the members of the class, and the teacher must decide where he is going to aim. If he caters for his top few then the duller children will find the work difficult, but if he 'lowers his sights' he risks holding back and

boring his brighter children. Boredom usually leads to mis-
behaviour. Thus he must have rigid rules and insist that they are
conformed to, because wherever he 'sets his sights' he must
surely frustrate one section or another of his class, and by doing
so lose their attention and interest.

The modern primary school aims to awaken the child's
interest in learning, to view each child as an individual and cater
for him accordingly, to give each child the opportunity to
produce creative work and to experience the satisfaction which
accompanies the achievement of original and valuable work. The
school in no way aims to compare one child with another, but
only to compare what each child is now producing with what he
has previously produced. As well as producing children who are
capable of working at their own intellectual level, the school must
give emphasis to the development of the child in other fields –
self-confidence, initiative, responsibility, respect and understanding for others are among the things we hope to foster.

Some years ago, when I was teaching eleven-year-old children
in an informal 'discovery-centred' atmosphere, I found myself
in a position to compare formal and informal methods. The
class had spent its third year in the junior school under the care
of a teacher who was considered first class, and who had taught
in the school for more than thirty years. Her discipline was
rigid and the children were certainly made to work hard during
their year with her. When they were moved up to my class
they obviously missed the props which the authoritarian regime
had provided. Although they knew their tables by heart and
never failed to dot their 'i's or cross their 't's, they were unable to show initiative – broken pencils caused consternation
and they needed permission before they made any move. These
children had remembered what they had been taught but were
unable to use that knowledge except within the context in which
it had been learned; they lacked the confidence to progress, to
investigate. Their learning was a passive acceptance of knowledge
and it took many weeks to arouse a desire in them to find out.
Their written work was presented beautifully but lacked origin-
ality; they had acquired some knowledge but had not yet learned
what is, to my mind, the most important factor in junior education – learning how to learn.

What then are modern primary-school methods? This question cannot be simply answered, as there is certainly no one new method. The modern theme is a mixture of approaches in which the best of the old methods have been retained – in the most individually centred classrooms there are frequent occasions when it is preferable to teach the class as a unit. Basically the modern primary school recognizes that the child is an individual with his own personal wants and needs. I don't want to engage in a philosophical discussion on the implications of 'needs', 'felt needs' and 'wants', but obviously the more the child's needs and wants can be equated, the more likely the child is to engage actively in learning. Having recognized the child's individuality, the teacher using modern methods creates a teacher–child relationship which is special to that particular child and which pays attention to the child's own strengths and weaknesses.

In the good modern classroom one may see all the children at any one time working at the same subject but at their own level, or more often, the children working at a number of different subjects. Whichever method is employed the teacher, whilst not perhaps appearing to, will be in complete control, not in a domineering way, but by quietly guiding and stretching and leading on. It is wrong to say that correction has no place in the junior school, though much of this is done quietly and individually. It may no longer be page after page of ticks and crosses, but the work is seen and the child encouraged rather than disheartened.

The weakness of arithmetic teaching in the past has been its emphasis on accuracy without understanding. In modern schools the children's work in mathematics is geared to an understanding of basic concepts. They are given the chance to discover for themselves; yards, feet and inches are no longer just columns in a textbook, but are real things that the children use in their practical mathematics about the school. Structural apparatus is used to give more reality to number, and I have found that children taught the new mathematics leave the junior school with a much stronger understanding of basic mathematical concepts. Of course the critics claim this accumulation of knowledge is haphazard and accidental, but in reality it is the result of a carefully planned but flexible course. Let us take as an example the teaching of area – most of my generation were probably taught to memorize 'L × B = A (sq.in.)' and then we could 'do' the necessary pages in our textbook; the modern primary-school child arrives at this formula by experimenting with squared paper, cutting out shapes, blocks of wood, etc., and the teacher helps him to realize the relationship existing between 'A and L and B'. Thus although he arrives at the same formula he does so with understanding: the equation is meaningful and he is able to use it and adapt it to many related problems. I do not claim that there is no place for much of the routine of arithmetic, but that the child who learns his number tables by building them up and gaining insight into the mathematics behind them is far better equipped than the child who is only capable of mere mechanical recitation. Of course some children leave the junior school not understanding 'area' or not knowing their tables, but how many previously left 'knowing' but not understanding?

A frequent attack is made on modern teaching of English – the cry is that children cannot punctuate nor spell correctly. The implication is that one cannot be encouraged to write freely and creatively and at the same time write grammatically and spell correctly. This has not been my experience – the teacher's influence is always present, mistakes are pointed out and help given with spelling. This is not done in a formal way with forty children listening to a lesson on the correct use of 'their' and 'there', when perhaps all but a handful understand already. How much better that those who do have difficulty are helped individually and at the appropriate time.

The teaching of English and arithmetic is no longer restricted to periods set aside during the day; it spills over into the variety of subjects which make up the modern junior-school curriculum. In many schools these subjects merge as the children work, together or separately, on projects, pursuing their own interests but carefully led by their teacher so that their knowledge is broadened. They are trained to use the library which is increasingly becoming of great importance in many schools, so that they know how to gather information; then they record this information in a variety of ways. It has been my experience that the most progressive teachers set standards as high as their more formal colleagues, and careless work is not likely to be accepted whatever the form of recording.

There are good and bad schools whatever the mode of education, just as the standard of teachers varies; to provide examples of schools where modern methods are poorly used does nothing to prove that modern methods are ineffectual. Throughout the country schools are producing pupils whose confidence, reasoning powers, spirit of cooperation and sympathy, together with their academic standards, pay tribute to the modern methods being used at the present time. These children are alert and have a zest for learning that stands them in good stead as they move through the secondary stages of education.

# Basil Bernstein
## Education Cannot Compensate for Society

**Basil Bernstein studied at the London School of
Economics and taught at the City Day College, London,
from 1954 to 1960. He is now professor in the sociology
of education at the University of London Institute of
Education, and head of the Sociological Research Unit.
He is the author of numerous articles on education,
with particular reference to language and social class.**

Since the late 1950s there has been a steady outpouring of papers
and books in the United States which are concerned with the
education of children of low social class whose *material* circumstances are inadequate, or with the education of black children
of low social class whose *material* circumstances are chronically
inadequate. A vast research and educational bureaucracy
developed in the United States, which was financed by funds
obtained from federal, state or private foundations. New educational categories were developed – 'the culturally deprived',
'the linguistically deprived', 'the socially disadvantaged'; and
the notion of 'compensatory education' was introduced as a
means of changing the status of the children in these categories.

Compensatory education emerged in the form of massive
pre-school introductory programmes like Project Headstart,
large-scale research programmes such as those of Deutsch in the
early 1960s and a plethora of small-scale 'intervention' or
'enrichment' programmes for pre-school children or children in
the first years of compulsory education. Very few sociologists
were involved in these studies, because education was a low-
status area. On the whole they were carried out by psychologists.

The focus of these studies was on the child in the family and
on the local classroom relationship between teacher and child.
In the last two years one can detect a change in this focus. As a

result of the movements towards integration, and the opposed movement towards segregation (the latter a response to the wishes of the various Black Power groups), more studies are being made in the United States of the *school*. Rosenthal and Jacobson's classic study, *Pygmalion in the Classroom*, drew attention to the critical importance of the teacher's expectations of the child.

In this country we have been aware of the educational problem since the writings of Sir Cyril Burt before the war. His book, *The Backward Child* (1937), is probably still the best study we have. After the war, a series of sociological surveys and public inquiries into education brought this educational problem into the arena of national debate, and so of social policy. Now in Wales there is a large research unit, financed by the Schools Council, concerned with compensatory education. Important research of a different kind is taking place in the University of Birmingham into the problems of the education of Commonwealth children. The Social Science Research Council and the Department of Education and Science have given £175,000, in part for the development of special pre-school programmes concerned to introduce children to compensatory education.

One university department of education offers an advanced diploma in compensatory education. Colleges of education also offer special courses under the same title. So it might be worth a few lines to consider the assumptions underlying this work and the concepts which describe it, particularly as my own writings have sometimes been used (and more often abused) to highlight aspects of the general problems and dilemmas.

To begin with, I find the term, 'compensatory education', a curious one for a number of reasons. I do not understand how we can talk about offering compensatory education to children who in the first place have not, as yet, been offered an adequate educational environment. The Newsom Report on secondary schools showed that 79 per cent of all secondary modern schools in slum and problem areas were materially grossly inadequate, and that the holding power of these schools over the teachers was horrifyingly low. The same report also showed very clearly the depression in the reading scores of these children, compared with the reading scores of children who were at school in areas which were neither problem nor slum. This does not conflict with the findings that, on average, for the country as a whole, there has been an improvement in children's reading ability. The Plowden Report on the primary schools was rather more coy about all the above points, but we have little reason to believe that the situation is very much better for primary schools in similar areas.

Thus we offer a large number of children, both at the primary and secondary levels, materially inadequate schools and a high turnover of teaching staff; and we further expect a small group of dedicated teachers to cope. The strain on these teachers inevitably produces fatigue and illness and it is not uncommon to find, in any week, teachers having to deal with doubled-up classes of eighty children. And we wonder why the children display very early in their educational life a range of learning difficulties.

At the same time, the organization of schools creates delicate overt and covert streaming arrangements which neatly lower the expectations and motivations of both teachers and taught. A vicious spiral is set up, with an all too determinate outcome. It would seem, then, that we have failed to provide, on the scale required, an *initial* satisfactory educational environment.

The concept, 'compensatory education', serves to direct attention away from the internal organization and the educational context of the school, and focus our attention on the families and children. 'Compensatory education' implies that something is lacking in the family, and so in the child. As a result, the children are unable to benefit from schools.

It follows, then, that the school has to 'compensate' for the something which is missing in the family, and the children are looked at as deficit systems. If only the parents were interested in the goodies we offer, if only they were like middle-class parents, then we could do our job. Once the problem is seen even implicitly in this way, then it becomes appropriate to coin the terms 'cultural deprivation', 'linguistic deprivation', and so on. And then these labels do their own sad work.

If children are labelled 'culturally deprived', then it follows that the parents are inadequate; the spontaneous realizations of their culture, its images and symbolic representations, are of reduced value and significance. Teachers will have lower expectations of the children, which the children will undoubtedly fulfil. All that informs the child, that gives meaning and purpose to him outside of the school, ceases to be valid or accorded significance and opportunity for enhancement within the school. He has to orient towards a different structure of meaning, whether it is in the form of reading books (*Janet and John*), in the form of language use and dialect, or in the patterns of social relationships.

Alternatively the meaning structure of the school is explained to the parents and imposed on, rather than integrated within, the form and content of their world. A wedge is progressively driven between the child as a member of a family and community, and the child as a member of a school. Either way the child is expected, and his parents as well, to drop their social identity, their way of life and its symbolic representations, at the school gate. For, by definition, their culture is deprived, and the parents are inadequate in both the moral and the skill orders they transmit.

I do not mean by this that in these circumstances no satisfactory home–school relations can take place or do not take place; I mean rather that the best thing is for the parents to be brought *within* the educational experience of the schoolchild by doing what they can do, and this with confidence. There are many ways in which parents can help the child in his learning, which are within the parents' spheres of competence. If this happens, then the parents can feel adequate and confident both in relation to the child and the school. This may mean that the contents of the learning in school should be drawn much more from the child's experience in his family and community.

So far I have criticized the use of the concept of 'compensatory education', because it distracts attention from the deficiencies in the school itself and focuses upon deficiencies within the community, family and child. We can add to these criticisms a third.

This concept points to the overwhelming significance of the early years of the child's life in the shaping of his later development. Clearly there is much evidence to support this view and to support its implication that we should create an extensive nursery-school system. However, it would be foolhardy indeed to write off the post-seven-years-of-age educational experience as having little influence.

Minimally, what is required *initially* is to consider the whole age period up to the conclusion of the primary stages as a unity. This would require considering our approach, at any *one* age, in the context of the whole of the primary stage. This implies a systematic, rather than a piecemeal, approach. I am arguing here for taking as the unit, not a particular period in the life of the child – for example, three to five years, or five to seven years – but taking as the unit a stage of education: the primary stage. We should see all we do in terms of the sequencing of learning, the development of sensitivities within the context of the primary stage. In order to accomplish this, the present social and educational division between infant and junior stages must be weakened, as well as the insulation between primary and secondary stages. Otherwise gains at any one age, for the child, may well be vitiated by losses at a later age.

We should stop thinking in terms of 'compensatory education' but consider, instead, most seriously and systematically the conditions and contexts of the educational environment.

The very form our research takes tends to confirm the beliefs underlying the organization, transmission and evaluation of knowledge by the school. Research proceeds by assessing the criteria of attainment that schools hold, and then measures the competence of different social groups in reaching these criteria. We take one group of children, whom we know beforehand possess attributes favourable to school achievement; and a second group of children, whom we know beforehand lack these attributes. Then we evaluate one group in terms of what it *lacks* when compared with another. In this way research unwittingly underscores the notion of *deficit* and confirms the *status quo* of a given organization, transmission and, in particular, evaluation of knowledge. Research very rarely challenges or exposes the social assumptions underlying what counts as valid knowledge, or what counts as a valid realization of that knowledge. There are exceptions in the area of curriculum development; but, even here, the work often has no built-in attempt to evaluate the changes. This holds particularly for educational priority area 'feasibility' projects.

Finally, we do not face up to the basic question: What is the potential for change within educational institutions as they are presently constituted? A lot of activity does not necessarily mean *action*.

I have taken so much space discussing the new educational concepts and categories because, in a small way, the work I have been doing has inadvertently contributed towards their formulation. It might, and has been said, that my research – through focusing upon the subculture and forms of family socialization – has also distracted attention from the conditions and contexts of learning in school. The focus on usage of language has sometimes led people to divorce the use of language from the substratum of cultural meanings which are initially responsible for the language use. The concept 'restricted code', to describe working-class speech, has been equated with 'linguistic deprivation' or even with the 'non-verbal' child.

We can distinguish between uses of language which can be called 'context-bound' and uses of language which are less context-bound. Consider, for example, the two following stories which the linguist, Peter Hawkins, constructed as a result of his analysis of the speech of middle-class and working-class five-year-old children (see *Language and Speech*, April–June 1969). The children were given a series of four pictures which told a story and they were invited to tell the story. The first picture shows some boys playing football; in the second the ball goes through the window of a house; the third shows a man making a threatening gesture; and in the fourth a woman looks out of a window and the children are moving away.

Here are the two stories:

1. Three boys are playing football and one boy kicks the ball and it goes through the window the ball breaks the window and the boys are looking at it and a man comes out and shouts at them because they've broken the window so they run away and then that lady looks out of her window and she tells the boys off (Number of nouns: 13. Number of pronouns: 6).

2. They're playing football and he kicks it and it goes through there it breaks the window and they're looking at it and he comes out and shouts at them because they've broken it so they run away and then she looks out and she tells them off (Number of nouns: 2. Number of pronouns: 14).

With the first story, the reader does not have to have the four pictures which were used as the basis for the story, whereas in the case of the second story the reader would require the initial pictures in order to make sense of the story. The first story is free of the context which generated it, whereas the second story is much more closely tied to its context. As a result, the meanings of the second story are implicit, whereas the meanings of the first story are explicit.

It is not that the working-class children do not have, in their passive vocabulary, the vocabulary used by the middle-class children. Nor is it the case that the children differ in their tacit understanding of the linguistic rule system. Rather, what we have here are differences in the use of language arising out of a specific context. One child makes explicit the meanings which he is realizing through language for the person he is telling the story to, whereas the second child does not to the same extent.

The first child takes very little for granted, whereas the second child takes a great deal for granted. Thus, for the first child, the task was seen as a context in which his meanings were required to be made explicit, whereas the task for the second child was not seen as a task which required such explication of meaning. It would not be difficult to imagine a context where the first child would produce speech rather like the second.

What we are dealing with here are differences between the children in the way they realize, in language use, what is apparently the same context. We could say that the speech of the first child generated universalistic meanings, in the sense that the meanings are freed from the context and so understandable by all; whereas the speech of the second child generated particularistic meanings, in the sense that the meanings are closely tied to the context and would be only fully understood by others if they had access to the context which originally generated the speech. Thus universalistic meanings are less bound to a given context, whereas particularistic meanings are severely context-bound.

Let us take another example. One mother, when she controls her child, places a great emphasis on language, because she wishes to make explicit, and to elaborate for the child, certain rules and reasons for the rules *and* their consequences. In this way the child has access through language to the relationships between his particular act which evoked the mother's control, and certain general principles, reasons and consequences which serve to universalize the particular act.

Another mother places less emphasis on language when she controls her child and deals with only the particular act; she does not relate it to general principles and their reasoned basis and consequences.

Both children learn that there is something they are supposed, or not supposed, to do; but the first child has learned rather more than this. The grounds of the mother's acts have been made explicit and elaborated; whereas the grounds of the second mother's acts are implicit, they are unspoken.

Our research shows just this. The social classes differ in terms of the *contexts* which evoke certain linguistic realizations. Many mothers in the middle class (and it is important to add not all), relative to the working class (and again it is important to add not all by any means), place greater emphasis on the use of language in socializing the child into the moral order, in disciplining the child, in the communication and recognition of feeling. Here again we can say that the child is oriented towards universalistic meanings which transcend a given context, whereas the second child is oriented towards particularistic meanings which are closely tied to a given context and so do not transcend it. This does not mean that working-class mothers are non-verbal, only that they differ from the middle-class mothers in the *contexts* which evoke universalistic meanings. They are *not* linguistically deprived, neither are their children.

We can generalize from these two examples and say that certain groups of children, through the forms of their socialization, are oriented towards receiving and offering universalistic meanings in certain contexts, whereas other groups of children are oriented towards particularistic meanings. The linguistic realizations of universalistic orders of meaning are very different from the linguistic realizations of particularistic orders of meaning, and so are the forms of the social relation (for example, between mother and child) which generate these. We can say, then, that what is made available for learning, how it is made available, and the patterns of social relation, are also very different.

Now, when we consider the children in school, we can see that there is likely to be difficulty. For the school is necessarily concerned with the transmission and development of universalistic orders of meaning. The school is concerned with making explicit – and elaborating through language – principles and operations as these apply to objects (the science subjects) and persons (the arts subjects). One child, through his socialization, is already sensitive to the symbolic orders of the school, whereas the second child is much less sensitive to the universalistic orders of the school. The second child is oriented towards particularistic orders of meaning which are context-bound, in which principles and operations are implicit, and towards a form of language use through which such meanings are realized.

The school is necessarily trying to develop in the child orders of relevance and relation as these apply to persons and objects, which are not initially the ones he spontaneously moves towards. The problem of educability at one level, whether it is in Europe, the United States or newly developing societies, can be understood in terms of a confrontation between (a) the school's universalistic orders of meaning and the social relationships which generate them, and (b) the particularistic orders of meanings, and the social relationships which generate them, which the child brings with him to the school. Orientations towards 'meta-languages' of control and innovation are not made available to these children as part of their initial socialization.

The school is attempting to transmit un-commonsense knowledge – i.e. public knowledge realized through various 'meta-languages'. This knowledge is what I have called universalistic. However, both implicitly and explicitly, school transmits values and an attendant morality, which affect the contents and contexts of education. They do this by establishing criteria for acceptable pupil and staff conduct. These values and morals also affect the content of educational knowledge through the selection of books, texts and films, and through the examples and analogies used to assist access to public knowledge (universalistic meanings). Thus, the working-class child may be placed at a considerable disadvantage in relation to the *total* culture of the school. It is not made for him; he may not answer to it.

The universalistic functions of language – where meanings are less context-bound – point to an 'elaborated code'. The more particularistic functions point to a 'restricted code'. Because a code is restricted it does not mean that a child is non-verbal, nor is he in the technical sense linguistically deprived, for he possesses the same tacit understanding of the linguistic rule system as any child. It does not mean that the children cannot produce, at any time, elaborated speech variants in *particular* contexts.

It is critically important to distinguish between speech variants and a restricted code. A speech variant is a pattern of linguistic choices which is specific to a particular context – for example, when talking to children, a policeman giving evidence in a court, talking to friends whom one knows well, the rituals of cocktail parties, or train encounters. Because a code is restricted it does not mean that a speaker will not in some contexts, and under specific conditions, use a range of modifiers or subordinations, or whatever. But it does mean that where such choices are made they will be highly *context-specific*.

This 'concept code' refers to the transmission of the deep-meaning structure of a culture or sub-culture – the 'core' meaning structure.

'Codes', on this view, make substantive the culture or sub-culture by controlling the linguistic realizations of contexts critical to socialization. Building on the work of Professor Michael Halliday (see *Educational Review*, November 1969) one can distinguish four critical contexts:

1. The regulative contexts: these are the authority relations where the child is made aware of the moral order and its various backings.

2. The instructional contexts: here the child learns about the objective nature of objects and acquires various skills.

3. The imaginative or innovating contexts: here the child is encouraged to experiment and re-create his world on his own terms and in his own way.

4. The interpersonal contexts: here the child is made aware of affective states – his own and others.

In practice these are interdependent, but the emphasis and contents will vary from one group to another. I suggest that the critical orderings of a culture or subculture are made substantive, are made palpable, through the way it realizes these four contexts linguistically – initially in the family. If these four contexts are realized through the predominant use of restricted speech variants with particularistic – i.e. relatively context-tied – meanings, then the deep structure of the communication is controlled by a restricted code. If these four contexts are realized predominantly through elaborated speech variants, with relatively context-independent – i.e. universalistic – meanings, then the deep structure of communication is controlled by an elaborated code. Because the code is restricted, it does not mean that the users *never* use elaborated speech variants. It only means that such variants will be used infrequently in the process of socializing the child in his family.

The 'concept code' makes a distinction similar to the distinction which linguists make between the 'surface' and 'deep' structure of the grammar. Sentences which look superficially different can be shown to be generated from the same rules.

The linguistic choices involved in a précis will be markedly different from the linguistic choices involved in a self-conscious poem. These in turn will be markedly different from the linguistic choices involved in an analysis of physical or moral principles; or different again from the linguistic realization of forms of control by a mother. But they may all, under certain conditions, reveal that speech codes – either restricted *or* elaborated – underlie them.

Now because the subculture or culture, through its forms of social integration, generates a restricted code, it does not mean that the resultant speech and meaning system is linguistically or culturally deprived, that the children have nothing to offer the school, that their imaginings are not significant. Nor does it mean that we have to teach the children formal grammar. Nor does it mean that we have to interfere with their dialect.

There is nothing, but nothing, in the dialect as such, which prevents a child from internalizing and learning to use universalistic meanings. But if the contexts of learning – for example, the reading of books – are not contexts which are triggers for the children's imaginings, are not triggers for the children's curiosity and explorations in his family and community, then the child is not at home in the educational world. If the teacher has to say continuously, 'Say it again, dear; I didn't understand you', then in the end the child may say nothing. If the culture of the teacher is to become part of the consciousness of the child, then the culture of the child must first be in the consciousness of the teacher.

This may mean that the teacher must be able to understand the child's dialect, rather than deliberately attempting to change it. Much of the context of our schools is unwittingly drawn from aspects of the symbolic world of the middle class, and so when the child steps into school he is stepping into a symbolic system which does not provide for him a linkage with his life outside.

It is an accepted educational principle that we should work with what the child can offer; why don't we practise it? The introduction of the child to the universalistic meanings of public forms of thought is not 'compensatory education'; *it is education*. It is not making children middle class; how it is done, through the implicit values underlying the form and content of the educational environment, might.

We need to distinguish between the principles and operations that teachers transmit and develop in the children, and the contexts they create in order to do this. We should start knowing that the social experience the child already possesses is valid and significant, and that this social experience should be reflected back to him as being valid and significant. It can only be reflected back to him if it is part of the texture of the learning experience we create. If we spent as much time thinking through the implications of this as we do thinking about the implications of Piaget's development sequences, then it would be possible for schools to become exciting and challenging environments for parents, the children themselves and teachers.

We need to examine the social assumptions underlying the organization, distribution and evaluation of knowledge, for there is not one, and only one, answer. The power relationships created outside the school penetrate the organization, distribution and evaluation of knowledge through the social context. The definition of 'educability' is itself, at any one time, an attenuated consequence of these power relationships.

We must consider Robert Lynd's question: 'knowledge for what?' And the answer cannot be given only in terms of whether six-year-old children should be able to read, count and write. We do not know what a child is capable of, as we have as yet no theory which enables us to create sets of optimal learning environments; and even if such a theory existed, it is most unlikely that resources would be available to make it substantive on the scale required. It may well be that one of the tests of an educational system is that its outcomes are relatively unpredictable.

# Arthur Razzell
# Reflections on Primary Education

Arthur Razzell has taught in primary schools and been
headmaster of a new primary school on a large council
housing estate in London. Subsequently he was
lecturer in the London University Institute of
Education and a member of the steering committee of
the Schools Council. He has written many television
scripts for primary schools and books on primary-school
mathematics. At present he is senior project officer in
the Department of Educational Research at the
University of Lancaster, carrying out a study of the
middle years of schooling. He is the author of
'Juniors: A Postscript to Plowden' (1968).

I was attending a junior school when the Hadow Report on the
primary school was as old as the Plowden Report is today – a
massive, solid, three-tiered, raspberry coloured, brick building
which will doubtless outlast my earthly span by many decades.
It was on the asphalt playground of this school that I fought
my fantasy battles against Hitler and Mussolini just as the
previous generations had fought against Kruger and the Kaiser.
It was in the classrooms of this school that I learned of the
greatness of Clive and Nelson, the vastness of our Empire, the
loyalty of our Dominions, how to read, write and do sums. It
was in the hall of this school that I learned 'Land of Hope and
Glory', 'The British Grenadiers' and where I daily paid my act
of homage to the old boys who failed to survive Passchendaele
and the rest. Never, at the going down of the sun or in the
morning, did we fail to remember them. It was the spirit of this
school which sent me cheerfully as a volunteer into the Royal
Navy, and I mock them not, they carved too deeply into my
nature for me ever to underestimate their profound influence.

On the morning of 20 January 1935, along with all the other ten-plus children in the neighbourhood, I sat the Junior County Scholarship Examination. Looking back on it after the passing of more than thirty years I find it odd that such a system should ever have existed, for no matter how brilliantly or how badly we all answered the examination questions exactly 80 per cent of us were ordained to fail! Odder still that, had I lived one mile to the south, on that particular morning I would have taken an examination set by another L E A where 89 per cent of their ten-plus children were foredoomed to failure. But perhaps oddest of all is the fact that in some parts of the country this strange process still continues. Choose your home in x-shire and your child will have a 40 per cent chance of attending a 'selective secondary school'; move to parts of y-shire and your child's chances may drop as low as 8 per cent. It is a sobering and frightening thought that in the closing decades of this momentous century a strong and realistic case can be made to show that we have an educational system designed to produce a majority of failures, and that if this were not the case then the system would break down.

In 1931 the Hadow Report said profoundly: 'Conditions have changed and we cannot escape the consequences of the change.' We can say that again. Change of the magnitude we are now experiencing is a positive invitation to the critics to have a field day, and although any sector of the education service can be made to appear rather dreadful by any reasonably informed observer, the primary schools clearly offer the best target for derision. They suffer the disadvantage of lacking many friends in high places. The overwhelming majority of education officers were teachers in the secondary field; so are the majority of lecturers in colleges and schools of education. Whilst this in no way debars them from having a good and sympathetic understanding of the work of the primary schools, they are by nature and inclination more ready to comprehend the needs of the secondary schools, and this is understandable.

There has been an overall shortage of teachers for the past thirty years, but this has imposed itself most strongly on schools for the younger children – and the results of that will not be eliminated for many years. There has been a shortage of money for the past thirty years and, whilst almost every educationist would agree that the primaries have not had their fair share of the financial cake, few have been anxious to bring pressure on the holders of the purse strings for a more reasonable distribution of the funds. By tradition, the primaries have been forced to accept the necessity of working with larger classes than any other sector of the educational service, despite the fact that they have had to cope with the full range of intellectual ability in overcrowded rooms. This was recognized as wrong by the Hadow Committee as far back as 1931, but the educational organizers took a contrary view at that time and have continued to do so. There is also little doubt that the primary schools have produced the most vigorous pioneers and, in many cases, shown the greatest readiness to accept change. However, it is only in the past decade that changes of a significant nature have begun to affect a substantial number of schools.

When we consider the changes which have been taking place in primary education we need to set it against this background of shortage of money, frequent shortage of reasonable accommodation, classes universally agreed to be too large, and in many cases shortage of adequate staff. Before we look in detail at the nature and quality of the changes which are taking place let me state that in my opinion they very, very rarely indicate wild and reckless experiment on the part of primary teachers. To my mind there is no question of a thoughtless profession undertaking educational vivisection on a generation of trapped and helpless youngsters. Secondly, I believe that although in a few cases changes have been rapid enough to justify the use of the word 'revolution', they are not yet either swift enough or radical enough to measure up to the changes which have been affecting society at large. Since both these claims represent personal value judgements, I must attempt to justify them.

Let me start with the actual content of the primary curriculum, for in this area there is likely to be general agreement over the need for change. It is not sound economics to prepare the nation's children for a way of life which has already ceased to exist. In the Edwardian days there was a need for an adequate supply of counting-house clerks and literate workmen. Today there is a need for men and women with more sophisticated skills. In the disciplines of science and mathematics alone there is sufficient change to make it clear that it would not be a wise use of time to spend the six years of primary education learning a little oversimplified nature study and practising computational skills in arithmetic. The explosion of knowledge in other disciplines is no less dramatic and primary teachers are seeking ways of making the basic concepts in these areas of knowledge familiar to their children. A decade will pass before their children have left school and teachers are concerned not simply with current changes – the decimalization of money, followed by the change-over to full metrication, the closing of the last national pit in the Rhondda, North Sea gas and men on the moon – but also with significant changes at the rock-face of knowledge.

However, it is not just the *content* of the curriculum which is changing. There is a move away from our traditional methods of instructing children. Our society today feels differently about people and this is reflected in the way the good hospital bothers about a patient's fears and anxieties, the way social workers are more sympathetic to those in need and the general feeling of indignation when examples of bureaucratic insensitivity are made public. Primary schools are also reflecting this changed attitude towards people, in their concern for the individual child. There are few primary teachers today who rely on the technique of mass instruction as their main teaching method. They are increasingly concerned with the growth of knowledge and skills in individual children and are aware of the many problems which can so easily affect a child's learning potential. It is no longer good enough to sit back in the comfortable chair and listen to forty children reading round the class; diagnostic testing of the retarded and backward pupils and the planning of remedial programmes to help them are essential. It is equally important to see that the fluent reader is guided towards the good books which will lead him on and that the pupils of average ability are not neglected. To work in this way on so many different fronts is much more demanding; it calls for more patience, more effort and energy and much greater professional skill. There is also a much greater element of anxiety, guilt and uncertainty involved, for no generation of teachers has ever faced change of this magnitude before. Most teachers have to live with the knowledge that they simply haven't the time to keep up to date on all that is happening and that the inevitable pressures have resulted in neglect of some children.

Although many would feel that educational research has been rather neglected in this country or not wisely planned, numerous research findings are being published. Whilst no teacher could read them all in detail, there are not many who fail to keep themselves reasonably informed. The whole field of language learning, linguistics and reading is coming into focus and the primary teacher wants to know the possibilities and to consider the dangers. Should he teach environmental studies, social studies, or continue to work in the separate disciplines – or are there other alternatives? What are the social and educational advantages of having an unstreamed school compared with the school which attempts to stream by presumed academic abilities? What problems are involved in making a change-over? How can home–school relationships be improved, and to what extent should the school take advantage of twentieth-century travel and engage in studies beyond the normal classroom environs? Primary teachers are thinking and working in these and numerous other areas but the work is frequently so demanding that there is little time to stand back and consider what is actually happening. In the field of primary mathematics alone the teacher faces a choice of over seven hundred different texts and many hundreds of different teaching aids – small wonder if at times some choices and decisions are made without adequate time to reflect.

It is a sobering thought that those who work in the primary schools have virtually no say in the selection of entrants to colleges of education or in any aspect of their course of training; yet these students will be their future colleagues! Frequently head teachers have no opportunity of selecting suitable teachers to serve in their schools (one body sent along to fill one vacancy was the normal drill when I was a head) yet, despite this, so many of our schools are doing marvellous work. As I visit primary schools in many parts of the country there is so much to see that is already good. Although the British economy seems insecure, never have our children been so well fed, well clothed and well cared for. Never has discipline in the schools been so relaxed or the children so responsive and eager to tackle the work in hand.

As you observe the speed with which our society is rebuilding and remodelling its banks and supermarkets to meet the needs of the 1970s, spare the occasional moment to glance at some of those buildings constructed for the 'education of children of the deserving poor'. It is inside many of those buildings that our nation is preparing to meet the needs of the twenty-first century.

# Part Four
**Secondary**

# Peter Mauger
## Selection for Secondary Education

Peter Mauger read modern history at Cambridge and taught in one independent and three secondary modern schools. He was headmaster of Nightingale Secondary School, London, for ten years, and is now head of the Education Department, Coventry College of Education. He has written articles on children's comics, teaching unstreamed classes and curriculum reform in the secondary school, and is co-author, with Leslie Smith, of 'The British People, 1902-1968' (1969). He is also a member of the editorial board of the educational journal 'Forum'.

'The Government ... believe it is wrong to impose a uniform pattern of secondary organization on local education authorities. ... Where a particular pattern of organization is working well and commands general support the Secretary of State does not wish to cause further change without good reason.'

Thus the Department of Education's Circular 10/70, withdrawing the comprehensive circular 10/65 and issued with admirable speed a mere twelve days after the Conservative election victory in June 1970. Subsequent developments have been muddied by contradictory policies both at the centre and among local education authorities. But while expressing a general approval of comprehensive education, Mrs Thatcher has also stated unequivocally her intention to retain 'schools of a wide range of character', as she said when speaking to the North of England education conference in January 1971. Simultaneously she has blocked or discouraged several plans for comprehensive reorganization, including one in her own borough of Barnet, and as Caroline Benn points out in the 1971 edition of her annual survey of reorganization plans, many others have been delayed or undermined.

Mrs Benn also points out that in 1960 fewer than 5 per cent of secondary-school children attended comprehensive schools, while in 1971 the estimated percentage is 35 and in 1972 will be 39. However, it must be borne in mind that even before 1970 the momentum of reorganization was declining, a process which Circular 10/70 was designed to abet. In addition, many schools which are nominally comprehensive are heavily creamed by the competition of grammar or other selective schools. The whole of our school system is deeply affected by the continued process of selection for secondary education. Selection procedures during the last year in the junior school are still very much the order of the day; most children undergo them, almost all are affected by them.

The emphasis on selection for secondary education began in 1907 with the regulations governing free places in secondary schools. As the century progressed and the demand for the limited number of grammar-school places grew, L E A s began to employ educational psychologists who developed various forms of verbal reasoning tests. Psychologists believed that they could devise tests free from environmental influence, because of the then commonly held theory that children were born with an innate intelligence determined by inherited genes, that the I Q of a child could be determined at an early age with considerable precision and that the figure so determined would remain fairly constant throughout school life. These tests could thus be used to predict academic success.

During the Second World War it became obvious that the educational system had resulted in an enormous wastage of ability. The armed services, to supply their needs, had to train vast numbers of young men to carry out expert jobs – for instance, R A F pilots and navigators – hitherto the prerogative of public-school boys. This experience, and the great wave of democratic aspirations unleashed by the war, led to demands for the recasting of the whole educational system. These demands were to be only partly fulfilled.

In 1943 a government committee produced a report which was to play an important part in shaping post-war educational policy. This was the Norwood Report. The committee chairman was Sir Cyril Norwood, formerly headmaster of Harrow. The Norwood Report stated revealingly the currently accepted orthodoxy among educational administrators about grammar-school children, technical-school children and the rest, decently camouflaged under the title of secondary-modern school children. These stereotypes are described in the following extract from the report:

The pupil who is interested in learning for its own sake, who can grasp an argument or follow a piece of connected reasoning, who is interested in causes, whether on the level of human volition or in the material world, who cares to know how things came to be as well as how they are, who is sensitive to language as expression of thought, to a proof as a precise demonstration, to a series of experiments justifying a principle. ... Such pupils, educated by the curriculum commonly associated with the grammar school, have entered the learned professions or have taken up higher administrative or business posts. ...

Again the history of technical education has demonstrated the importance of recognizing the needs of the pupil whose interests and abilities lie markedly in the field of applied science or applied art. ... He often has an uncanny insight into the intricacies of mechanism whereas the subtleties of language construction are too delicate for him. ...

Again, there has of late years been recognition ... of still another grouping of pupils. ... The pupil in this group deals more easily with concrete things than with ideas. He may have much ability, but it will be in the realm of facts. He is interested in things as they are; he finds little attraction in the past or in the slow disentanglement of causes or movements. ... His horizon is near and within a limited area his movement is generally slow, though it may be surprisingly rapid in seizing a particular point or in taking up a special line.

Had the committee sought evidence from psychologists whose views were no longer the oversimplified ones of the inter-war period, they might have paused before publishing such pernicious nonsense. As Rex Knight, Professor of Psychology at Aberdeen University, said in 1950 of the Norwood Report:

The only connection between psychologists and this innovation [the tripartite system] is that they have vigorously attacked the ground on which it was recommended by the Norwood Committee. Thus they have pointed out that there is no evidence for the suggestion that a definite stage of growth begins at about the age of eleven, or for the crucial statement that the three types of school correspond to three distinct types of mind, clearly discernible among children of eleven (in C. H. Dobinson, ed., *Education in a Changing World*, 1951).

The Report went on:

In a wise economy of secondary education pupils of a particular type of mind would receive the training best suited for them and that training would lead them to an occupation where their capacities would be suitably used.

The old prayer comes to mind – *God bless the Squire and his relations, and keep us in our proper stations.*

It is hardly surprising that people with such an artificial, compartmentalized notion of human beings should advocate apartheid in secondary education (though apparently they viewed with equanimity the thought of their own sons in public schools mixing with the other two types – or perhaps public-school boys all belong to the first type?) At all events, by a convenient coincidence there happened to be three types of secondary school corresponding to these three categories; and the 1944 Education Act resulted in the tripartite system as we know it today. IQ tests formed the basis of the selection procedures, backed up by arithmetic and written English attainment tests.

Even if it were true that intelligence was a fixed entity, un-affected by a child's environment since birth and capable of being measured accurately by IQ tests, there would still be powerful arguments against segregation of adolescents into different types of secondary school. But it would be difficult to find many educational psychologists – and more difficult still to find social scientists – who now hold the theory of intelligence on which the whole basis of selection at eleven is founded. As Professor P. E. Vernon has pointed out (*Bulletin of the British Psychological Society*, October 1968), there is no way of con-clusively separating inherited from acquired intelligence. All the psychologist can do is to observe the effectiveness of the child's behaviour or thinking as developed up to that time through the interaction of the genes and the stimulation pro-vided by the environment.

Recent research has supported what common observation suggests, that a child's attainment at eleven will be largely determined by his environment and experiences and may well change radically thereafter. A child who is given security by a happy home environment, who is stimulated by the interest and approval shown in his development, discoveries and explorations, and who is able to express himself through the growth of a wide vocabulary, will develop much more of his inherent conceptual and perceptual abilities than one starved in these respects.

Anxiety of parents for the success of their children is one factor contributing to success or failure in the eleven-plus examination. Another is the availability of grammar-school places in different parts of the country and even the same area. Although the worst disparities have ended with the coming of the comprehensive school, many remain. Among those London Boroughs which have established few comprehensive schools, for example, the percentage of thirteen year olds attending grammar schools in January 1970 varied from 7·9 in Barking and 13·6 in Newham, to 30·7 in Harrow and 32·5 in Barnet. A similar situation prevails elsewhere, though now more within than between local education authorities.

It is clear that tests based on a now discredited theory of intelligence are a most inefficient and unfair method of selection, even for its present purposes. They have also had serious adverse effects on primary-school education. But for selection at eleven-plus, there would be no need for streaming. Many more schools would follow the example of those who place more emphasis upon discovery and inquiry by the children than on mass instruction in the three 'r's and on preparing them to put down the 'right' answers to problems. There would be more time to help children with their individual difficulties and to enable them to develop as unique persons, rather than pressing them into a common mould. It is remarkable how many primary schools have refused to restrict their curriculum to the demands of the eleven-plus; but this must not obscure the fact that most primary schools regard it as a very high priority to get as many of their pupils as possible into grammar schools. One can hardly blame them when one considers the pressures of parents who realize the career advantage of a grammar-school place.

The growing unpopularity of the eleven-plus has led to modification of selection procedures in most L E As mainly by the abandonment of attainment tests in English and arithmetic. The use of verbal reasoning tests, however, remains almost universal, and greater weight is placed on teachers' assessments. This has the advantage that the child is not judged merely on the results of one day's examinations; but it has serious drawbacks. Someone has to standardize the teachers' assessments, pressure from the most articulate parents becomes more acute, and it is more difficult for a teacher, more often than not of middle-class origins, to judge fairly between a cooperative, neatly uniformed and polite child with a good vocabulary and a child from a home environment that has given him none of these outward appearances of intelligence. It is likely that it is the former child who will be recommended for the grammar school, a telling revelation of the fact that grammar schools are as much socially based on conventional middle-class values as they are faithful to the traditions of academic excellence.

The claim that these L E As have done away with the eleven-plus is nonsense; selection is simply being carried out in a different and even more subjective and class-biased way. These arguments about the best and fairest ways to select, about how to minimize strain on children, about how to avoid adversely affecting the primary-school curriculum, are all beside the point. What really should be discussed is: why select at all? If we reject the Norwood argument that there is a type of child with genes that fit him for a grammar-school education, what are we left with? That grammar-school places have to be filled somehow, and no one has yet found a better way to fill them than the present system. Behind the clarion cries of the elitists about the need to maintain standards and to educate the most intelligent for leadership, lies the unspoken assumption that children who have had the most advantageous start in life should be chosen for the schools that undeniably provide the greatest opportunities for interesting and well-paid careers.

Research has shown beyond a shadow of doubt that working-class children are grossly under-represented in grammar schools. J. W. B. Douglas, for example, estimates that 54 per cent of upper middle-class children but only 11 per cent of lower manual working-class children attend grammar schools (*Studies in British Society*, ed. J. A. Banks, 1969).

These figures alone are strong enough arguments for the abolition of maintained grammar schools and direct grant schools. If, after all these years of experiment in selection procedures, they can't do better than this, the sole valid reason for the maintenance of selection at eleven would be that only the maintenance of grammar schools can ensure a sufficient supply of well-educated citizens.

But this is exactly what the selective process and the existence of selective schools prevents. The nature of the tests encourage obedience, conformity, convergent thinking (there is only one right answer). The child who asks awkward questions, whose mind goes off at a tangent, the original divergent thinker is less likely to be selected. If selected, he is less likely to succeed at G C E O- and A-level, with their emphasis again on rote learning and convergent thinking. Either he has to conform, which warps the development of his creative qualities, or he won't do very well. This is bad educationally and bad for a country which, at a time of the greatest technological and social changes that the world has yet known, depends as few others on the development of the abilities of *all* its citizens, and of many and diverse kinds of ability.

To sum up: the tripartite system, and the selection processes necessitated by it, came into being on pseudo-psychological grounds that were no longer held even at the time it was introduced. The predecessors of the Black Paper polemicists succeeded in preserving a class-biased and elitist system of secondary education at a time when there was a massive demand and need for the democratization of all forms of Britain's political, economic and social life.

The results have been rigid streaming in the junior, and even the infant, schools; a narrowing of the curriculum in both, with an excessive emphasis on the three 'r's at the expense of the development of children's natural initiative, curiosity and desire to find out; strain on children, parents and teachers; drilling and coaching in tests in order that some shall pass an examination and most shall fail – surely the antithesis of education; tests based on an incorrect hypothesis, incorrectly placing 20 per cent of children even by their own terms of reference; and finally the creation of an elite in the grammar schools and resentment or under-confidence, apathy or hostility to school work in the secondary modern schools. Those who still support selection, despite the evidence, have to face the fact that they are also supporting rejection – rejection of four out of every five children.

The case for abolishing selection at eleven is unanswerable. The replacement of selective by comprehensive schools will not by itself guarantee a curriculum more suited to the needs of adolescents; but only a nation-wide system of comprehensive schools can make possible changes in the curriculum of both the primary and the secondary schools so that talent can be developed to the full and every child helped to grow as an individual with different and unique qualities.

# Dennis Marsden
## The Comprehensive School: Labour's Equality Machine

**Dennis Marsden went from a Huddersfield grammar school to Cambridge University, an experience he has described in 'Breakthrough' (ed. R. Goldman, 1968). With Brian Jackson he carried out a survey of his contemporaries from Huddersfield's grammar schools, published as 'Education and the Working Class' (1962), concluding that the grammar school must give way to a less restrictive form of education. In 1969 he published 'Mothers Alone', a study of poverty and the fatherless family. He now lectures in sociology at the University of Essex.**

The weaknesses and vacillations of Labour's comprehensive reorganization strategy reveal that leading Labour politicians have not yet agreed on the aims of reorganization, nor have they grappled with the problem of how political aims can be turned into good educational practice. By 1970, the comprehensive policy was in ruins, and the Party had been branded as inept in its attempt to 'interfere politically' with a matter best left to professional educators. Of course fair treatment for school-children will ultimately depend on how teachers behave in the classrooms. But the truth is that Labour did not interfere *enough* with the framework of education, and with the maldistribution of resources between schools, sectors of education, regions, neighbourhoods and families. Instead, the comprehensive school was allowed to appear an equality machine, which by itself would reduce and smooth over educational and societal inequalities.

The strategy was to try to give the impression that the policy of comprehensive reorganization was a response to an over-whelming electoral and technological demand for comprehensive schools, which would develop more fully the nation's resources of talent. But the actual planning and execution of reorganization and redistribution of educational resources were handed over to local authorities, without central drive or guidance. As a result, by 1970, five years after Circular 10/65 had asked local authorities to submit plans for reorganization, only 10 per cent of secondary schoolchildren were in schools unskimmed by selection, and the rate of opening new comprehensives was dropping (information from C. Benn and B. Simon's survey reported in *Half Way There*, 1970). Moreover, first reports of the ethos of the new schools seemed to hold little promise of the achievement of a more egalitarian society through comprehensive education.

The strategy was thus a failure at two levels: the politicians had not tried hard enough; but also the schools had not initially responded to the politicians' confused and over-sanguine intentions.

The Labour Party's formal commitment to comprehensive education conceals disagreements of aim which appear even in differing interpretations of the rallying call for 'equality of opportunity'. The left has laid the stress on 'equality' in a democracy where power would be widely diffused through local participation. The centre, on the other hand, has aimed for 'opportunity' in a meritocracy, where there would be rule by the intelligent, rather than the rich, few.

As early as 1925 the Labour Party Conference adopted a resolution seeking to 'create amongst children the qualities and outlook essential to citizens of a Cooperative Commonwealth'. Similar resolutions were debated and some were passed at subsequent Conferences. These political ideals found a more concrete educational expression through the National Association of Labour Teachers (now the Socialist Educational Association), who advocated a framework of 'common' or community schools where there would be positive unstreaming, a common core curriculum and flexible teaching methods. Supporters of such community schools have insisted that in them children's talents will be developed more fully – but only through drastic changes away from the restrictions of the academic curriculum and grammar-school ethos towards a more open and flexible school structure.

In the early years of the first post-war Labour government there was no evidence from working community schools, and Labour politicians and even theoreticians of the left such as G. D. H. Cole remained unconvinced of the need or possibility of such a radical reshaping of education. In so far as they supported comprehensive schools they adopted what might be called a 'social engineering' approach. Cole wrote that the schools should be 'designed to give every child a chance, but at the same time to avoid the creation of a new class structure based on intelligence'. In his ideal school 'differences of curriculum and standard in the classroom are combined with participation in mixed activities on the playgrounds, in clubs and societies and in any sort of out of school activity'. ('Education and Politics: A Socialist View', *Year Book of Education*, 1952). That is, social rather than educational change was to be achieved by 'social engineering', *around the existing curriculum and school structure*, rather than, as NALT wanted, through a change in the structure and ethos of education itself.

Still more recently comprehensive schools have won limited support from moderates in all parties on the grounds that large schools with a balanced ability intake may offer more opportunity and be more efficient in the use of scarce specialist teaching resources. Dr Rhodes Boyson, an avowed Conservative and 'meritocrat', and himself the headmaster of a large comprehensive school, wrote in 1968 that he believed a comprehensive system was desirable on the grounds of efficient teaching; but he doubted the social claims for comprehensive education, and it was 'essential that comprehensive schools maintained and, if possible, strengthened the academic tradition [of the grammar and public schools] whilst offering it to an increased proportion of the age group' ('Threat to Tradition', *Crisis in the Classroom*, ed. N. Smart, 1968).

Thus, under the flag of comprehensive education have sailed supporters of a number of different persuasions, ranging from egalitarians of the left through social engineers to meritocrats of the right, who view the traditional academic curriculum and the grammar school ethos from totally different standpoints. And a glance at the history of Labour's failure of nerve reveals that many Labour politicians at both national and local level have, overtly as meritocrats or covertly as social engineers, supported the continuation of grammar school traditions. As a result comprehensive reorganization has been slowed down and distorted by struggles *within* the Labour Party at national and local level.

We can now see why the first comprehensive schools were not an integral part of a post-war egalitarian legislative programme. The Labour leadership accepted the coalition White Paper on education with its rationale of different 'types' of abilities, and only minority pressure kept open a loophole in the 1944 Education Act by preventing the formal specification of tripartitism. It is arguable that Labour could have given a lead to public opinion and that, at the minimum, 'multilateral' (heavily streamed comprehensive) schools could have been introduced in 1945. The grammar schools had not yet become preparatory schools for higher education, and their limited and class-biased entry meant that on the whole working-class interest in gaining grammar-school places was still relatively weak. But the party leadership was not ready and the moment passed.

Through the loophole in the 1944 Act and against strong pressure from the conservative Ministry civil servants, a few local authorities pressed ahead with comprehensives, but the schools had an uphill struggle against competition from existing grammar schools.

It is unlikely that the principle of equality alone would ever have won its way into national party policy at any time after the immediate post-war period. However, sociological and psychological evidence mounted to show that the grammar schools were wasting the nation's brains in a tight economic situation, and that in addition the unpopular eleven-plus examination was inefficient and indeed invalid. So by 1964 it seemed that a comprehensive 'efficiency with equality' programme was tailor-made for the new science and technology image of the Wilson government.

Yet the Labour leadership seems to have retained a loyalty to the grammar school which put them in the schizophrenic position of wanting grammar and comprehensive education at the same time. Wilson, following Gaitskell, tried to present comprehensive schools as 'grammar schools for all', promising in

1963 that the grammar school would be abolished only over his dead body. A TV broadcast before he lost the 1970 election revealed no change in his standpoint. Roy Jenkins saw comprehensives merely as a bridge between secondary modern and grammar schools. And Anthony Crosland, who was in charge of implementing Labour's comprehensive commitment, adopted an explicitly social engineering approach, claiming both social and academic benefits for the comprehensive school but at the same time maintaining that the abolition of streaming would be 'against common sense'. There seems little evidence that the leadership ever fully understood, let alone sympathized with, the case for community schools.

External evidence supports the view that Circular 10/65 was actually the policy of the 'permanent politicians' of the Department of Education and Science, and was accepted by Labour for lack of adequate preparation before taking office and to paper over the splits within the Party over tactics.

Perhaps the Circular was expected to work. Labour claimed an electoral mandate for comprehensives, and successive Education Secretaries claimed to detect a 'groundswell', 'a running tide' and 'progress down the road' towards the abolition of selection. But according to *New Society* in October 1967, although 52 per cent of the population said they were in favour of comprehensive schooling, in another question 46 per cent chose grammar schooling for their child and only 16 per cent a comprehensive school. In a further question, in fact, 76 per cent wanted to retain grammar schooling and only 15 per cent were against it. As David Donnison commented, this was not a vote for comprehensives so much as a massive rejection of the secondary modern school.

Circular 10/65 gave further time for the polarization of opinion, and time was not on Labour's side. The public's dislike of the eleven-plus *examination* was not a rejection of eleven-plus *selection* as such, and resentment has diminished and disappeared with the continuing change to new and less obtrusive (but more unfair) systems of sorting by verbal reasoning tests, 'guided' parental choice and head-teachers' opinions, all of which favour the middle-class child.

Admittedly to pursue a policy alternative to Circular 10/65, resources would have been needed to persuade local authorities to build a new secondary-school system. Yet in spite of the economic crisis, expenditure on education has continued to rise rapidly. The conclusion is unavoidable that the Labour leadership lacked not resources but the vision and courage to establish priorities and to make unpopular and difficult decisions which would attack the existing maldistribution of educational rewards and privileges.

Thus, in the early comprehensive debates, the question of 'neighbourhood schools' raised in an acute form the wider problems of the unequal distribution of educational and cash resources between areas, regions and families. But Labour politicians took fright and left the Conservatives the opportunity to make it appear that the comprehensive programme created, rather than merely reflected, such inequalities. Labour fluffed the issue by quietly dropping the neighbourhood-school idea, allowing it to appear that careful adjustments of school catchment areas and intakes would solve everything. In effect the comprehensive school was saddled with the impossible task of becoming an equality machine to overcome the consequences of Labour's timidity in educational policy and in other fields as well. The Conservatives were justified in their accusations that this social engineering approach was doctrinaire, for unlike the community school the policy was not educational in its own right.

The issue of redistribution was further evaded when local authorities were handed, without comment or guidance, the hot potatoes of drawing the catchment areas and deciding on the degree of restriction of parental choice of schools. And throughout, the D E S officials behaved as if the comprehensive schools would always 'coexist' with a predominantly bipartite system. Circular 10/65's pretence of local involvement and local government's responsiveness to local needs was shown up as a sham. Far from the blossoming of a hundred flowers, the result of this lack of central guidance was an information and power vacuum at local level, where sets of party councillors who knew little about comprehensive education were in the hands of Local Education Officers who might or might not support comprehensives. In my own locality the grammar-school hall was packed with middle-class parents to hear a platform including not only the grammar-school heads but also some secondary-modern heads, a brigadier and a bishop who told the meeting to 'Thank God for the grammar schools'. Yet 6000 leaflets inviting council-estate parents to a discussion of comprehensive education brought only ten parents.

In these circumstances a committed Education Officer or individual councillors could be very influential in moulding a plan, and the interests of working-class parents were not adequately defended. Moreover plans produced often by reluctant and ill-informed committees were hardly the quickest or the best from any ideological standpoint.

When we peer through the dust raised by the political debate we find that discussion of comprehensive schemes has largely neglected the possibility that the schools will have their own internal dynamic, irrespective of what their supporters or opponents claim. In a politically delicate situation, constrained by the tightening eighteen-plus bottleneck, and staffed largely by teachers educated under the bipartite system, the new comprehensive schools at first showed a desire to compete with the grammar schools by entering very large proportions of their pupils for examinations. Some schools overtly preserved an archaic grammar-school ethos, one for example having first-year streams identified by the Greek letters of the word *gnothisautos*. In 1961 Robin Pedley found that nine-tenths of comprehensive schools gave children an academic ranking-order in class, and in 1965 the NFER research on comprehensives discovered that only 4 per cent were using complete non-streaming.

Yet Benn and Simon reported in *Half Way There* that by 1968 22 per cent of schools were using broad mixed-ability organization, and Robin Pedley reported in 1969 that 38 per cent of the long-established schools in his survey were 'operating in unstreamed situations to a greater or lesser extent', while the proportion of these schools ranking children in class had dropped to half. So there is support for Benn and Simon's view that the narrowly meritocratic emphasis on streaming and academic results which has characterized the first comprehensive schools will be a temporary phase, and that as comprehensive education becomes more widespread the internal dynamic of reorganization should begin to assert itself.

These early disappointments for egalitarians emphasize that the community and the meritocratic schools represent quite different ideals, whose achievements cannot properly be compared. Apart from the absence of enough true community schools, above all, meritocrats and egalitarians will want to evaluate education, even the 'development of talent', by different criteria. The educational arguments and specialist evidence are by now relatively obscure; and there will always remain some methodological problems and imperfections which will provide a loophole of objection, however nit-picking, for an opponent of particular findings. Research can illuminate the debate but will not enable us to choose between different visions of society.

It is unfortunate that one much-quoted piece of research by a supporter of the comprehensive school, Dr Julienne Ford's *Social Class and the Comprehensive School* (1969) is misleading in its suggestions that comprehensive schools will fail to develop talent or promote social mixing as much as the bipartite system. Dr Ford's survey constructed an 'ideal type' of comprehensive almost solely from the social engineering statements of Anthony Crosland. This was then tested against a London comprehensive almost certainly lacking the full ability range of pupils and of a crudely meritocratic structure where no attempts were made to promote social mixing across rigid streams. The research design is further invalidated by the fact that 'working-class' children who go to grammar schools are frequently of quite different social backgrounds from children who attend comprehensives, even where parental occupations are similar.

The best 'comprehensives' we have to date are in fact the primary schools. NFER research has shown that non-streaming has social advantages and no academic disadvantages but that it will only work if it is an expression of and not a constraint upon, teachers' approach and methods. This finding shows the undesirability of direct government control of the internal organization of primary or secondary schools such as is practised in Scandinavia.

Ironically, the Conservative election victory in 1970 has reopened the comprehensive issue, for the swing to Labour at local level may make the leadership responsive to pressures for changed and more positive policies. The establishment of more comprehensive schools has apparently won some support: recent figures in a poll which correctly asks the question whether respondents prefer the comprehensive system to the continuation of grammar *and* secondary modern schools show 46 per cent for comprehensives as opposed to 37 per cent in favour of bipartitism (*Comprehensive Education*, no. 14. Spring, 1970).

Comprehensive schemes once established have proved difficult to dismantle, if not to subvert. The Conservatives' reaction has therefore been to permit comprehensive schools in areas where the established grammar schools are not threatened, and otherwise to try to cool the issue. Mrs Thatcher withdrew Circular 10/65 and said that there would be little cash for secondary-school building because of the crying needs of the primary schools, to which Labour should have paid more attention. As a result, while Mrs Thatcher's opponents have been able to accuse her of rejecting several schemes for comprehensives on 'doctrinaire' Conservative grounds, there have been few major clashes. However, the impact of the switch to primary-school building has so far been cushioned by the provision of cash for raising the school-leaving age. We can therefore expect more serious clashes over comprehensives from 1973 onwards, when reorganization will be starved of funds.

We can now see that if we are ever to approach a truly comprehensive system, the next Labour government has a dual task in educating *its own* supporters, and providing a strong central definition of comprehensive education. Above all, a policy of comprehensive reorganization only makes sense in the context of a programme of redistribution in other areas of policy, in income, wealth and housing, with a range of positive discrimination towards poorer areas to bring them up to acceptable standards. Central government can also go a long way in establishing a democratic system of relationships within the schools, through the system of school governors. But the more radical proposals for a revolution of the ethos of our secondary education must still face the problem of how to foster a corresponding 'cultural revolution' among the teaching profession, upon whom will rest the ultimate responsibility for achieving the comprehensive principle.

# Brian Simon
## Streaming and Unstreaming in the Secondary School

**Brian Simon is Professor of Education at the University of Leicester. He has written and edited many books on the history of English education, on the comprehensive school and on educational psychology in the Soviet Union. Some of these are: 'The Common Secondary School' (1955), 'Studies in the History of Education, 1780-1870' (1960), 'Educational Psychology in the USSR' (edited with Joan Simon, 1963), 'Education and the Labour Movement, 1870-1920' (1965) 'Halfway There' (with Caroline Benn, 1970) and 'Intelligence, Psychology and Education: A Marxist Critique' (1971). He has been first co-editor and then editor of the educational journal 'Forum', since its inception in 1958.**

The movement for unstreaming has in recent years met with strong opposition from traditionalist writers on education. For example, *Black Papers Two* and *Three* (1969, 1970) contained several articles which sharply attacked the movement for abolishing or modifying the system of streaming. The Black Papers, indeed, appeared to link unstreaming with comprehensive education, student unrest and the permissive society as all leading to anarchy, or egalitarianism run wild.

It should be noted, however, that the attack on unstreaming concentrates on secondary schools, although the movement started in primary schools and has since spread to all types of secondary, including grammar, schools. We now know that children undergo no sudden change at eleven, so this process is natural. The modification of streaming at the secondary stage is motivated by the same factors as at the primary stage. What, then, is behind this movement? What is it all about?

Streaming developed as a 'system' throughout the state

schools, both primary and post-primary, in the 1920s and 1930s, to reach its peak in the early 1950s. Its origins can be traced to the beginning of the century, but it was particularly the re-organization of elementary schools into junior and senior following the Hadow Report of 1926 that made this practically a universal method of internal school organization.

The rigid method of grouping adopted was based on the theory that intellectual potential was largely determined by heredity, that it was fixed and unchanging and that it could be accurately assessed at an early age. On this basis, streaming was clearly defensible. The aim was to achieve homogeneous classes of roughly the same level of ability, and to teach the class as a class. In the 1920s or 1930s this theory was scarcely questioned in Britain, and streaming was adopted because it seemed the 'obvious' method of internal school organization. Certainly no research of any kind was carried out to discover whether other methods of grouping might prove superior.

Teachers began to abolish streaming when they lost faith in this theory of intelligence. It was specifically the research of such men as the Canadian physiologist Hebb, of Piaget on concept formation, of Luria on the role of language in mental development, which led to the breakdown of the old theories of intelligence. Intelligence is now defined very differently, as 'a fluid collection of skills whose development is demonstrably affected by early experience and subsequently by the quality and duration of formal education'. This quotation is taken from the massive survey of grouping procedures edited by Alfred Yates for UNESCO, and published under the title *Grouping in Education* (1966). It sums up the view most widely held by educational psychologists, in spite of the recent attempt by Arthur Jensen in the United States to reinstate the view that genetic factors have an overall and dominant influence on in-tellectual development (see e.g. *Harvard Educational Review*, Winter 1969).

It is now held that a child's intellectual skills and abilities, instead of being fixed by heredity, are formed in the process of his life and experience – in particular through his interaction with adults through the use of language. It follows clearly that the group of which a child forms part is itself a crucial factor in his development, providing him with stimulation in many different ways. The modern theory of intelligence makes it clear that to group children in different streams, A, B and C (and even down to N, O, P in a very large school) according to a prediction about future intellectual development, is no longer a viable procedure. The child's development will be determined, to some extent, by the specific group of which he forms part.

It was this point that was specifically stressed by the British Psychological Society in their important report *Secondary School Selection*, published in 1957. This report modified earlier theories of intelligence on the basis of recent research and pointed out the educational implications. The dangers of streaming, it stressed, 'are obvious'. Children

who are relegated to a low stream, to suit their present level of ability, are likely to be taught at a slower pace; whereas the brighter streams, often under the better teachers, are encouraged to proceed more rapidly. Thus initial differences become exacerbated, and those duller children who happen to improve later fall too far behind the higher streams in attainments to be able to catch up, and lose the chance to show their true merits.

This hypothesis was confirmed in the long-term research undertaken by J. W. B. Douglas, published in *The Home and the School* (1964). Douglas found that of children of similar measured ability, those placed in a high stream improved their performance in succeeding years, while those placed in lower streams deteriorated. He concluded that

streaming by ability reinforces the process of social selection. . . . Children who come from well-kept homes and who are themselves clean, well-clothed and shod, stand a greater chance of being put in the upper streams than their measured ability would seem to justify. Once there they are likely to stay and to improve performance in succeeding years. This is in striking contrast to the deterioration noticed in those children of similar initial measured ability who were placed in the lower streams. In this way the validity of the initial selection appears to be confirmed by the subsequent performance of the children, and an element of rigidity is introduced early into the primary-school system.

Streaming, in fact, was shown by this research to be a self-verifying hypothesis.

Many of these findings were supported by research in the later 1950s and early 1960s. It was found by H. Clark, for instance, that original stream placement (which might determine the child's entire future) was significantly affected by strictly irrelevant factors such as the child's age. Children born between September and December had a one in two chance of being placed in an A-stream, while those born at other times of a year had only a one in three or four chance (*British Journal of Educational Psychology*, November 1956). It was found by Brian Jackson that streaming was significantly related to social class, middle-class children being largely over-represented in A-streams and working-class children under-represented (and vice versa as regards the C-streams).* Early streaming was now seen as an arbitrary classification, but one which had a determining influence on the child's future development.

Early research in this country seemed to indicate the superiority of non-streaming; thus J. C. Daniels concluded, in an inquiry conducted in 1959 in two unstreamed and two streamed junior schools, that 'there appears to be fairly definite evidence that the policy of non-streaming, as compared with streaming, significantly increases the average I Q of children in the junior school by about three points' as well as significantly increasing the mean scores of pupils in reading and English tests as well as arithmetical attainment (*British Journal of Educational Psychology*, February and June 1961). At about this time the results of two Swedish research projects came to hand, and these also appeared to indicate that, over all, children gained from the non-streamed situation, and that the most advanced children at least did not suffer. It was largely on the basis of this research that the Swedish parliament passed a law making it illegal to stream pupils below the age of fifteen. At the same time research into the emotional development of children seemed to indicate that the non-streamed situation provided a better environment

*In a sample of over 7000 children in 228 four-stream primary schools, Brian Jackson found that 55 per cent of the A-stream and only 5 per cent of the D-stream came from professional and managerial families, and that 14 per cent of the A-stream and 32 per cent of the D-stream came from unskilled manual workers' families (*Streaming; An Education System in Miniature*, 1964, pp. 19–23).

for learning. Thus R. A. Pearce found in 1958 that the competitive atmosphere of streaming aggravated the ordinary frustrations of adolescence and that '... in any form where streaming, or anything else, gave a sense of failure or a reputation of inferiority, a decline in morale, effort and attainment was inevitable' (*Educational Review*, June 1958). Other researchers obtained similar results; for instance F. Chetcuti found that streaming tended to lower the morale in 'duller' streams, whereas in A-forms, while there was greater work satisfaction, there was a drop in 'group morale' or interaction (*Educational Review*, November 1961). C. J. Willig, whose research evaluated streaming from the angle of the child's social development, concluded that the unstreamed school provided a more effective environment for the development of positive social attitudes among children (*Educational Research*, February 1963). Thus by the mid-1960s a number of researches seemed to indicate the superiority of non-streaming from various points of view.

Most of the early British researches were concerned with the primary school. However, in the last few years there has been a tendency to modify or abolish streaming also in the early years of the secondary school. This is certainly linked to the move towards comprehensive education, which is itself an attempt to get away from what might be described as a functional system of education, one which siphons pupils at an early age in this or that direction in relation to future employment. But this may be done just as effectively by streaming within the comprehensive school as by a system of separate schools. It is to avoid, once more, too early differentiation and the inevitable waste connected with it that new forms of grouping are now being developed in secondary schools. At the same time this development, both in primary and secondary schools, represents a move away from the traditional teacher–learner syndrome, in which the teacher is active and the child passive. The current tendency, based on research into the nature of human learning, puts the emphasis on promoting self-directed learning by the child, on inquiry methods and the encouragement of initiative and creativity, on the flexibility of the classroom situation, on group and individual work as well as on class teaching. The teacher is seen as having the responsibility for structuring the child's learning experiences. This shift is a deliberate attempt to maximize the conditions of learning for all the children, and is based on modern knowledge both as to the nature of the child and of the process of learning itself.

There is, then, a clear rationale behind the modification of streaming in secondary schools as well. Research in this country already points to certain advantages. For instance, D. Thompson, head of Woodlands Comprehensive School, Coventry, carried out a long-term research project in his school, moving over to complete non-streaming in the first year in three stages. The decision to extend the abolition of streaming was taken at each stage on the basis of the research results which indicated that, as the school modified streaming, greater opportunities were given for the pupils to develop in ways which could not have been predicted at eleven. This applied both to pupils with high and with low I Qs. Thompson's conclusion was that the system of rigid streaming 'set a limit to the level of response of the majority of the pupils', that streaming 'produces or at least perpetuates undesirable social attitudes' and that the modification or abolition of streaming provides a better environment for both intellectual and social development (*Forum*, summer 1965). David Hargreaves, in his study of a secondary modern school *Social Relations in a Secondary School* (1967), confirmed Thompson's point on social attitudes. He found two subcultures at the secondary modern school he studied, the A- and B-streams which accepted the school's aims and cooperated, and the C- and D-streams which rejected them. 'It appears that at Lumley School,' he writes, 'and presumably at other similar schools, the development of opposing subcultures is an extreme form of this differentiation process, which is accentuated, if not caused by, the streaming system.' If this is so, the abolition of streaming might be effective in transforming pupils' attitudes, though, if such a policy were adopted, 'some fundamental rethinking about teaching methods would have to be made.' In many of the secondary schools which are modifying streaming in the early years, this rethinking is certainly taking place, spurred on by the new curriculum reform projects and by the increased availability of teaching aids which permit group work and the individualization of learning.

It cannot be too strongly pointed out that the abolition of streaming is in no sense linked with complacency about academic standards. On the contrary, it is an attempt to remove the limitations inevitably imposed by streaming, to find the means of allowing and encouraging each child actively to maximize his learning, under the guidance and control of the teacher. Certainly this involves difficult pedagogical problems – there is nothing simple or easy about it – but the strength of this movement shows that many teachers are ready and anxious to face this challenge. This is one of the most encouraging features of the present educational scene.

However, the UNESCO survey already referred to makes it clear that, over all, the abundant research on this question over the last forty years (much of it done in the United States) remains inconclusive. Some investigations have given results favourable to streaming, some to non-streaming, some show no significant differences. The very real difficulties in research on this topic are stressed. One problem is that of the criteria by which this change is evaluated, since the abolition of streaming means the substitution of different aims from those of the past. This point is explicitly recognized in the work of the National Foundation for Educational Research on this topic. Their initial research (published in the Plowden Report) appeared to indicate that streamed primary schools had a slight advantage in teaching traditional subjects (mechanical and problem arithmetic and English). Streamed and non-streamed schools, as they say, embody different philosophies. The former concentrate on more conventional lessons and are likely to be more 'traditional'. The latter present an 'apparent contrast', their teaching 'tends to place more emphasis on self-expression, learning by discovery and practical experience' (Plowden Report, vol. 2, 1967, pp. 572–3). A further report of the NFER (Joan C. Barker Lunn, *Streaming in the Junior School*, 1970), found 'no difference in the average academic performance of boys and girls of comparable ability and social class' in streamed and unstreamed junior schools. Their 'most striking finding', however, was that the emotional and social development of children of average and below average ability was strongly affected by streaming and non-streaming and by teachers' attitudes. It is probably the case that effectively to test the abilities developed in children in non-streamed schools requires new instruments only now being constructed. This conclusion is supported by an NFER follow-up report (Elsa Ferri, *Streaming: Two Years Later*, 1971), whose findings were broadly similar to those of Mrs Lunn.

There is a vast field for research into grouping, hardly yet explored. For instance, if streaming is abolished, on what principles should the children be grouped together? There is a wide variety of possibilities, each having different advantages and disadvantages. Then, where streaming is abolished, an almost infinite variety of classroom patterns may be developed – which of these are the most effective? Educational research has scarcely yet touched this vital question.

How to group children in schools is primarily an educational question, to be decided on educational grounds. Certainly research into psychology, sociology and even anthropology may be relevant and research findings should be taken into account. But the overall aim must be to achieve that method of grouping which provides the environment best suited to stimulating the cognitive and affective development of all the children. This has nothing to do with the bogy of egalitarianism; it is simply the only way of creating a viable educational unit. But it is also socially necessary. It is only by raising the general level of education among the population as a whole that the necessary basis is laid for raising the higher levels themselves.

Of course all decisions about so fundamental an issue have political overtones and implications – especially where it is a question of widening educational opportunity. But to attack these developments from the political angle – deliberately to ignore the educational rationale of new practices – implies that the motives of attack are suspect, or at least not disinterested.

The UNESCO report makes this point. The result of research on grouping, it states, 'is unlikely to modify significantly the attitudes of those who regard their prestige and security as being threatened by the implications of these findings'. This seems to hit the nail on the head. There is an urgent need to reexamine methods of grouping in schools and to make decisions based on clear and disinterested research. It is to be hoped that anyone genuinely concerned about the state of education in Britain will welcome changes made on this basis.

# Charity James
## Flexible Grouping and the Secondary-School Curriculum

As director of the Curriculum Laboratory at
Goldsmiths' College in the University of London from
1965 to 1970, Charity James worked with experienced
teachers planning educational reform in secondary and
middle schools. In 1970-71 she was visiting professor in
education at Boston University, and currently she has
a Ford Foundation award to encourage the development
of new methods in the middle years of schooling in the
United States. Her main publication is 'Young Lives at
Stake' (1968).

The children now in our schools may be present at the final
extinction of mankind. An educational system cannot solve the
problems of a society, far less of a species, but it can at least be
appropriate to the context in which young people are growing
up. The context today is a horizon of immense danger, on the
one hand, and seemingly limitless human development on the
other; in contrast, everyday life seems to offer few deep-felt
satisfactions and this is in part because we have not learned to be
satisfied with ourselves. Adolescents need an education which
they sense to be in accord with their own idealism and despair,
because it acknowledges the profound seriousness of the human
situation, the tenuousness of our hold on life, the inadequacy of
many of our social prescriptions. This does not mean, of course,
that it has to be doom-ridden; being concerned with truth, it can
be often warm, light-hearted and funny.

The new radical reforms in primary and secondary education
are sometimes represented as arising simply from observing
children and working with them. They should be seen also as
the outcome of a thorough-going reappraisal not only of our
context but also of human nature. In particular, they bring into

the schools a modern understanding of the character of human knowledge, the sources of human behaviour and the problems of human societies.

First, we have to recognize that we are an exploratory, creative, problem-solving species, whose best and most assured statements are necessarily contingent, speculative and partial. Today's facts, like today's norms, may well be tomorrow's errors. Knowledge is an activity, not a commodity. On the other hand, information, which is a commodity, is no longer a scarce one. It follows, therefore, both from the true nature of knowledge and from the present overwhelming quantity of information, that children should spend little time memorizing facts. Rather they should learn to scan and evaluate complex data.

Again, the attempt to separate thinking from feeling has been a disastrous failure; it is the whole person who learns and acts. From this, two changes follow, apparently disparate but closely interconnected. The first is that the expressive and creative arts become central to the curriculum rather than outlets for feeling only and so in some way inferior to the hard core of academic learning. But beyond this, the importance of the child's involvement in his work comes to be acknowledged. It is not true that provided you learn it does not matter how you feel about what and how you learn, since in large measure it is those feelings which determine what kind of person you become.

Finally, the reforms represent a vision of the school as a society grounded in the primacy of persons. This may sound facile, but I believe that a new understanding is involved, not a return to rank individualism, nor a synthetic sweetness which denies the need for truthful conflict, nor indeed the frequent tiresomeness, and worse, of human beings. The point is that equality alone is seen to be insufficient. It has become little more than a quantitative concept which was mounted to avert exploitation and has failed to do so. In the context of human jeopardy, the stress should be not on mere equality but on diversity. Men are born diverse, and everywhere are under pressure to become the same – only the local moulds are different, and often mutually exclusive. By welcoming the fact that people are different, have different pulses, talents, growth rates, physical build, interests, sexual ambitions, temptations, temperaments, even physical scales of perception, we have some hope of countering the in-built tendency of all modern large-scale organizations to quantify and depersonalize, which is one of the greatest threats to survival. More means worse only if it means more of the same.

In the new developments, flexible grouping of children and reform of curriculum are inextricably interwoven. Simply to unstream children and then teach them the old curriculum meets none of the requirements of our situation; nor is it enough to attempt a new curriculum while maintaining the same techniques. The class lesson, for instance, which attempts to keep thirty or forty children on the same hard tack, is extremely wasteful as a technique of communication. True, occasionally a teacher's magic may keep a whole class enthralled, and he should not be deprived of occasions to exercise his magic, nor they to enjoy it. But the normal basis of work becomes the small group or cluster of less than half a dozen, or the individual who is happy for the time being to work on his own. The teacher's activities are varied, demanding and interesting. He is a partner in formulating problems and hypotheses for resolving them, he gives access to resources or experiences which are needed, he explains the nature of evidence, he sorts out learning difficulties and at times he provides straightforward exposition where this is needed. All this can be done without denying the learner's need for autonomy in inquiry and problem solving.

With younger children, flexible grouping is relatively straightforward, but as they move to secondary schools, with specialist teachers, larger numbers and more sophisticated equipment, more complex planning is needed. The proposals which follow are the outcome of long-term consideration at the Goldsmiths' College Curriculum Laboratory by heads and other experienced teachers in conjunction with the permanent members of the unit, and are being used as a basis of innovation by a number of schools.

The aim is a mosaic, not a melting-pot. Adolescents need to be able to follow their own bent; they also have much to contribute to and gain from common enterprises. We have formulated a fourfold foundation of study based on the nature of the subject matter and the special requirements of the individual. First, we think young people should have the opportunity to work in an open situation, devoting themselves to problems of some complexity. This we call Interdisciplinary Enquiry (I D E) indicating by the name that the basic activity is inquiry (in the broadest sense of questioning, identifying problems, seeking explanations) and that study of major human problems will be meagre unless it draws on the resources of many disciplines, including the natural sciences and the creative arts. Young people work in 'clusters' for up to half the timetable, perhaps five forms blocked together with five teachers from different fields. Secondly, they need at times to work within the accepted limits of a discipline, and this will be in a group of the usual class size with the usual single teacher. There is also a growing tendency for teachers in allied disciplines to collaborate in something broader than their own subject but narrower than I D E, so they are already moving away from a rigid interpretation of a fourfold curriculum.

The two other bases for bringing children together are quite different, for they are not concerned with the content of study but rather with the varying requirements of individuals. Children have special interests which cannot always be met in I D E or in the ordinary study of a subject. They may need to go into the same material in greater depth, or they may want more out-of-the-way provision. Acknowledgement of special interests is vitally important in adolescence and should not be side-tracked into extra-curricular events; it may be particularly important for children with a very specialized talent but it has value for others also. For practical reasons of staffing, but also as a matter of policy, we propose that groups sharing special interests should cross age lines, as this broadens young people's social experience and their chance to learn from one another.

The same is true of the fourth aspect of the curriculum. Here the criterion is the learner's special needs: a child is blocked in something he wants or needs to do by some lack in his education. He needs coaching. Sometimes a group will be similar to a remedial set in a conventional school, but more successful children have special needs too, sometimes at a high level of work, and are held back by lack of diagnosis and special help. It is really extraordinary how little this has been recognized in secondary schools, especially when one considers how many children are ill, change schools or go through bad patches in learning and then want to catch up. It is here that the use of programming and technical aids, closely related to the diagnosis of individual difficulties, will probably be most fruitful.

These four bases for grouping might be called the macrocosmic aspects of flexible grouping in a diversified curriculum. Diversity is also the essence of I D E, for it is in the open, freewheeling work of I D E that one begins to see how narrow has been our concept of 'mixed ability'. Many clusters are based on friendship or shared interests, but there are times when the teacher can propose other constructive groupings. Negative mixed ability grouping, a refusal to divide children, is a refusal to do harm; but we need more positive concepts, and it should be a growing part of a teacher's skill and understanding to develop them, with the help of research.

Already Roda Amaria and her colleagues at the National Centre for Programmed Learning have shown that at quite ordinary tasks the best results are achieved when children of different I Q and appropriate personality are paired. Liam Hudson has shown the advantage given in our traditional education to the 'convergent' thinker, who is happiest doing what he has been told. Some modern searchers for talent invert the rank order and cherish only the child who can produce plenty of ideas of his own. This isn't just to change victims; it is surely to miss the whole point. In I D E young people can be engaged in very complex studies, perhaps looking at the biological and cultural aspects of growing up; or at the local environment, how it has changed, is changing and ought to be improved; or at human survival and the balance of nature; or at the influence of technological change on employment; or at love and hate; or at themselves as individuals and as a group; or at any other of a vast range of important questions which are open to them and their teachers. For this they need not only a variety of disciplines but a variety of dispositions. There is a place for the technically or intellectually inventive, for the person who can clothe an idea with examples or test it effectively, for the scholarly ferret, for someone who just feels there's something wrong somewhere but can't put his finger on it, for those who can contribute a clear analysis of data and for others who more readily make direct

personal statements in the arts. Young people who would otherwise be in a low stream can give a great deal; indeed their insights are often more penetrating than those of the academic
sprinter. In this microcosm of an open society all can be welcomed as they are, without any limits being set to what they
might become.

New developments of this kind in secondary schools are in
their infancy. They should not be treated as dogma, but they do
deserve to be allowed their early difficulties and growing pains.
One should not be sanguine that this will be granted them. Reforms with such radical implications for society disturb and
anger many people, for they run counter to an elderly regime with
intellectual and economic assumptions which belong to the past.
There are those, too, who think one can bring secondary education up to date by more superficial means, offering social justice
in the form of more examinatons for more children, adding
some visual aids, a soupçon of team teaching because it 'helps
the teacher to put on a better performance', and some social
education for those who have been tested and found wanting –
any coherent study of the human situation being viewed as a
waste of good learning time for those who expect later to manage
our affairs. Patching of this kind may seem to get our education
into the twentieth century. It will not help us to survive into the
twenty-first.

# Wyn Williams and John Rennie
## Social Education

Wyn Williams has taught in a secondary school in
Nigeria, in the extra-mural department of Makerere
University College, Uganda, and in the School of
Education at Nottingham University. Two years ago he
joined the Social Education Project and is now lecturer
in community education at Trent Polytechnic.
John Rennie taught for nine years in Manchester schools
before going to Nottingham to run the Social Education
Project. He is now the Local Authority Adviser in
Community Education at Hillfield, Coventry.

The school is a co-educational bilateral secondary school serving
one of the twilight areas of Nottingham: an old, long-established
area on low-lying land near to the River Trent, first developed
after the Enclosure Acts of the eighteenth century; an area of
small terraced houses and corner shops rubbing shoulders with
small factories, all grimy with smoke, inevitable in an area boun-
ded by the railway station to the north and the power station to
the south. The houses are often, though not always, substandard; the population includes many 'respectable' working-class
English and immigrant families, as well as the less 'respectable' –
the inadequate, the drifters, the lonely, the maritally unstable.

The redevelopment plan is phased over ten years in five stages.
Families are already moving out – those that can; some old
people have already been rehoused within the area – in an isolated block of flats too far away from shops and telephones;
nurseries and primary schools are being rebuilt or improved, and
head teachers cannot predict how many places they will have in
September this year.

The school is fairly new, built across the river amidst fields; the
buildings have recently been enlarged to accommodate increased

numbers created by the merging of a secondary modern school in the same area with the bilateral.

The class we have been working with this year is one of fourth-year leavers, fifteen year olds, a near 'bottom' stream. Above them in the school are the classes that stay for five years, taking G C E and C S E examinations, and above them there are those in the grammar school. The class have already been 'doing' Social Education for two years. During this time they have studied the groups they belong to, those that have most impact on them, like the peer group and the family. They have also looked at their school, interviewing the Head, the prefects, the caretaker, their fellow pupils, with particular reference to two points: how much of what these people do is by statutory obligation, so to speak, and how much is over and above the call of duty? In the process of these studies – or 'profiles' – the children have been given the opportunities to develop skills in observation and communication. In mock interviews they have tried to learn how to put people at their ease; they have then been placed in face-to-face situations with both peers and adults in and out of school. Today their class teacher and we have decided to introduce to them the problems which the redevelopment will create for their community. We do not give them a lecture; we do not outline the problems that we, or the sociologists, or the welfare services, think will be created. Simply we present to them two sets of figures:

Present population of the area:    14,500
Population after redevelopment:    5750

Immediately the questions are fired at us:

What happens to those who can't stay here?
Who is going to move?
How is it decided?
When will people have to go?
Supposing they don't want to go?

The questioning went on throughout the period; answers were not given by ourselves or the class teacher. We did not know. We made it clear that any answers must be found by us all together. The next step was to study the draft redevelopment plan, and the alternative proposals being suggested by various pressure groups. Over a period of weeks the group worked out what questions seemed to them to be the most important, and discussed how they could find out the answers. The class divided themselves into smaller groups of two or three children, each of which decided which aspect it most wanted to investigate.

They wanted to know how people in the area were reacting to the plan, particularly when it involved moving; they wanted to know about the rents of new houses or flats, about removal costs, about the cost of refurnishing new homes. Their investigations involved them in planning who they needed to talk to, what questions they needed to ask. They needed to go out of school, unsupervised, to interview people – local inhabitants, the town planning department, city councillors. They visited the exhibition mounted in the area by the planning department, and attended a public meeting on the redevelopment plan.

The work continued for two school terms (with two periods a week on the timetable). Out of it, apart from the amassing of information, and the experience of this kind of action survey work, came various proposals for action that they, as a group, would like to see initiated.

'We ought to show people what's going to happen. They don't seem to know or care.' One suggestion was for a mobile exhibition (as opposed to the official one mounted in a local Church Hall) which would tour shops, launderettes, pubs – places where people would be forced to notice it. Another suggestion was for posters, and one boy designed a cartoon/poster showing a family at the breakfast table and a bulldozer driving into the wall: WAKE UP NOW! The most ambitious suggestion was for an alternative redevelopment plan, which brought violent arguments over various proposals: one, for instance, that the area should be rebuilt with the same density of population by the simple expedient of new terraced houses to replace the old – rather than the 'garden city' type development visualized by the planners, with its low density, separate industrial developments, green open spaces and its eighteen shopping units to replace the existing 184 corner shops.

At this stage when the class have reached an indignation point of wanting to *do* something, the teacher also arrives at a critical point: to what extent can he allow the situation to continue to develop? To what extent can he allow, and to what extent will authority allow, the children to take the kind of action to which the work they have been doing has stimulated them? To what extent can they be allowed time to further their proposals?

Is it in fact part of the function of schools to provide for this kind of work at all? To provide for the children *in* school to become actively involved in the community in which they live, *not* in the form of the so-called 'community service' as propagated in so many schools, but in the form of action-surveys: i.e. the identification of community problems (through survey work) and the planning and initiation of action which seems to the children *themselves* relevant and necessary?

There is a great deal of lip-service paid in education circles to the concept of educating people to live in a democracy. The problem is that education for democracy can be interpreted to suit ones own concepts both of education and democracy. The most common effect of schools is to inculcate in its pupils, either implicitly or explicitly, the moral–social code accepted by Directors of Education, head masters–mistresses, school–teachers. Hierarchically organized schools (implicit) with school rules (explicit) and the complete lack of opportunity for children to be involved in decision-making, will not further the aim of creating a participating democracy. Community service – sending schoolchildren to help various groups of people predescribed as deprived, or less fortunate makes no effort to involve the children in identifying *for themselves* problems which exist within their own community.

Most schools would claim that their intention is to produce what used to be called 'good citizens': one of the problems lies in one's definition of a 'good' citizen – or a 'useful member of society'. Is such a person one who accepts without question the standard codes of behaviour; or is he one who questions the codes and comes to his own conclusions about them, who formulates his own code of behaviour?

One of the boys who took part in the action survey we have described, informed his class teacher that he had given up 'doing over' telephone kiosks. It transpired that as a result of the survey work he had suddenly realized the importance of a telephone box that worked to some members of the community (such as old people and mothers with sick children). 'And anyway,' he added, 'I'm not so bored now.' School work had at last proved interesting.

The Schools Council Project on Social Education has been an attempt to test, in practice, various beliefs: beliefs about the importance of community involvement and commitment; beliefs about the need for an awareness of community and the ways in which this may lead to self-awareness and a sense of identity; about the ability of groups within a community to work to bring about change; beliefs about the possibilities of training children in school – over a period of years – in the skills required to work as groups within their known community, to identify problems and to attempt to take action for change.

It is not of course claimed that by training groups of schoolchildren in this way major changes can be initiated. Such a school programme is visualized only as part of a widescale training programme aimed at all kinds of established (recognized) workers in the community as well as at all individual members of the community. The central concept of this doctrine, as developed by Richard Hauser (Senior Research Fellow in Social Planning at Nottingham University) is that of self-help: identification of problems, initiation of action, must come from *within* the community and not be imposed from *outside*: it must come from 'us' not 'them'. These beliefs came to be put to the test when the Schools Council agreed to sponsor the Social Education Project (1968–71).

The work in the four schools involved in the Project led us to conclude that certain factors need to be present if social education is to have a chance of making an impact within school. There must be an opportunity for a class of children to build up a close relationship with a teacher – preferably over a couple of years. There must be sufficient flexibility in the timetabling for work that cannot be given a subject label to find time. The time required will vary depending upon the stage which the children have reached. When they get to want to take action, then more time is needed and contact outside school is involved. However, the 'progressiveness' or otherwise of a school need not be a significant handicap.

Perhaps the greatest success from our point-of-view was achieved with the class whose action-survey work we have described above, in a school not committed to so-called progressive methods, with a low-streamed class of fifteen year olds from a deprived area. We describe the results here as successful, not because the work done was all of a consistently high standard, not because all the children were influenced – or even interested – by the work, but because a number of children were given, for the first time, opportunities for decision making, for working on their own, and because a significant number of them were influenced enough by the work, to want to take action about community problems that they had discovered.

The teacher of this particular class must take the greatest share of the credit for the success. He is a man who is committed to his work, who cares about his pupils, and who communicates these feelings to the children. What the Project provided was both a method of work and a theoretical framework which was in accord with this teacher's own beliefs, as well as the support of educational respectability provided by our Schools Council–University backing.

He, like us, is hopeful:

Speaking for myself I have no certainties, but I have a few hopes. I hope (with, I believe, some justification) that at least some of the pupils will retain interest in what goes on around them. Some of them will not forget that society consists of people and people can be influenced. Some are already planning to continue their involvement in affairs after they have left school.

Many schools faced with the problems created by the raising of the school-leaving age are searching desperately for a way of coping. Those that seize on Social Education as a way of occupying the school-leaving classes, without recognizing the beliefs and commitments that lie behind the scheme, and without recognizing the need for the process to develop over at least three years, are likely to be disappointed. Social Education is not a variation on social studies, liberal studies, civics, etc. It involves a belief in the need for social (and, by extension, political) change, and a belief in schools as part of the wider community rather than separate, perhaps hostile, entities. We believe that children can be trained to act as agents of change within their community, and our programmes of work, although they are developed according to the needs of particular pupils in particular environments, are devised with this objective in mind.

Experience in decision making, working on your own, development of self-awareness must necessarily precede action for change. Not all children will develop the same degree of awareness; not all of those who do develop an awareness will become involved in community action; but if we can bring some children to the point of such awareness, both of self and of community, then we shall have achieved our objective, so far as work in schools is concerned.

The problem then is that one must not stop here. Convincing schools that Social Education is important is only a small part of the work that needs to be done. Schools have always reflected society; they will not, of themselves, produce change. If social education in schools is to have any real, any lasting value, then it must be accompanied by similar programmes throughout the community.

# Donald McIntyre*
## Assessment and Teaching

**Donald McIntyre took degrees in mathematics and education at Edinburgh University, and then taught at Dunfermline High School, Hull University and Moray House College of Education. His research has included work on teacher's opinions and their perceptions of pupils, and on assessment techniques. He is co-author with Arnold Morrison of 'Teachers and Teaching' (1969) and 'Schools and Socialization' (1971). At present he is engaged on research, at Stirling University, into the training of teachers.**

It is easy to think of assessment as a part of the teacher's work quite separate from his teaching. During most of the term one gets on with the main job, but then tagged on at the end is the examination one has to give. At the same time, examinations have been widely attacked as having a harmful effect upon the work of both teachers and pupils. I shall argue, on the contrary, that assessment – whether by examinations or by other techniques – is an integral part of effective teaching and that attacks upon examinations as such have often been misdirected.

The value of our assessment practices can ultimately be judged only in relation to our educational goals. These are many, various and complex, but for present purposes it is useful to focus on two very general goals. On the one hand, the major explicit aim of most teachers is the furtherance of cognitive development: increasing pupils' knowledge, understanding and intellectual skills. On the other, a major implicit aim of the educational system is social selection, since the eventual position of a person in the social-class hierarchy is to a large extent deter-

*The writer wishes to acknowledge his debt to Arnold Morrison and Jack Duthie who have influenced his thinking on this subject.

mined by the way in which he is classified within this system. This essay will concentrate on the first of these aims, asking what sort of assessment practices are appropriate to it, to what extent these are our current practices and to what extent the short-comings of the present situation are due to the importance attached to social selection.

Effective teaching involves ensuring that pupils have a series of experiences from which they will learn as completely and quickly as possible. A major part of teaching is deciding, at each stage in a pupil's learning, what experience will be most useful for him next. In order to make appropriate decisions of this sort a teacher has to assess the pupil's present state: his understanding, difficulties, interest, frustration, etc. He has to know what information about the pupil is needed and relevant to his teaching objectives (which means he must first know what these are); he must be able to obtain this information efficiently and accurately; and he must be able to interpret and use the information once he has obtained it.

Assessment as a basis for making teaching decisions is neces-sary both from moment to moment in the classroom (Does $x$ understand what I have just said? Is $y$ listening?) and at much longer time intervals (What aspects of the subject is $z$ interested in? Has my approach with this group been too abstract so far? How many of this class have mastered 'area' sufficiently for them to be introduced to 'volume'?). Teachers have to depend very largely on their social skills of observing and interpreting other people's behaviour, skills which should therefore be trained to a higher level than is general in the population. But if they are to have sufficiently reliable information, this needs to be supple-mented by the use of more carefully planned and more objective assessment procedures. These may well include such instru-ments as attitude scales and sociometric questionnaires, but tests and examinations are perhaps the most important since they are most directly related to teaching objectives. The sorts of examination which are most useful – theoretical or practical, written or oral, essay or 'objective', in class or at home – depend on many factors in the teaching situation; there are no simple rules. The choice of an appropriate form of examination, and the design of that examination, require from the teacher a skilled and knowledgeable analysis of the information he needs and of the best way of obtaining it.

For teaching purposes, examinations are useful in so far as they provide information about how far each of the teacher's specific objectives have been attained by each individual pupil and by the class as a whole (e.g. about which pupils have understood each of the major concepts with which the course is concerned). They are also useful in so far as they reveal the nature of pupils' errors and misconceptions. The teacher needs these kinds of information both to continue the teaching of each pupil in a way appropriate to his needs and also to know what modifications in his teaching are desirable when dealing with future classes.

Teachers can easily underestimate their needs for information about their pupils. In an experiment carried out some years ago in the United States, psychologists provided teachers with various kinds of detailed information about individual pupils; as a result, the attitudes of teachers towards these pupils changed and there was a significant improvement during the following months in the relative attainments of these pupils. When, however, this experiment was recently repeated in Britain, there were no such changes. The explanation for this difference appeared to be that the British teachers had taken very little interest in the information provided; as one said: 'Oh, yes, that stuff you sent me; I wonder where I put it?'

One reason for this lack of concern for information may be that teachers do not appreciate the relevance of certain kinds of information. For example, although there is a good deal of evidence suggesting that the relationships among pupils in a class have a significant effect upon their learning, many teachers are uninterested in such relationships; as a result they tend not to know which pupils are most influential or which are unpopular, and often act on wildly mistaken assumptions about such things. A second reason for not wanting to know more about pupils is that teachers often think they know enough already. In all social relationships people tend to make oversimplified judgements of others on the basis of relatively little information. While this is to some extent inevitable, professional teachers should surely be expected to make only the most sophisticated of judgements about their pupils, since the consequences of their judgements are so important. But there is clear evidence that many teachers make stereotyped judgements of children; their use of social-class stereotypes, for example, has the result that working-class children tend to be allocated to streams, and to be taught, as if their attainments were poorer than they are.

Pupils are, or can be, active participants in the processes of collecting and using information. In the first place, it is important that the information which teachers feed back to their pupils should be such that it helps them to take purposeful action towards realistic learning goals. It has been experimentally demonstrated, for example, that the subsequent attainments of pupils who receive written comments appropriate to their individual examination performances tend to be superior to those of pupils whose teachers give them only grades or marks.

Pupils can also be active in giving information to their teachers. There is some evidence that they are better even than trained observers at evaluating the relative skilfulness of different teachers, and they are certainly in a better position than anyone else to say how they respond to various aspects of a teacher's behaviour. It is therefore a fortunate teacher who has established a relationship with his pupils in which they feel free to tell him which things they find helpful, useless or distracting. Pupils also know a great deal about their own learning difficulties and achievements which the teacher cannot know, and it seems obvious that their self-assessments could be of great value to him. But self-assessment is only likely to be of value in situations where pupils believe that the teacher is not concerned to evaluate and possibly condemn them, but is only concerned with teaching them.

Skilled assessment of the sort discussed so far is likely to contribute greatly to the effectiveness of teaching. But in our current educational practice, although we expend an enormous amount of time and energy on assessment, very little information is obtained which helps teachers to teach. Instead, we give pupils marks or grades, that is, we concentrate on *judging* them, on saying how 'good' or 'bad' they are, on putting them in an 'order of merit'. Assessment of this evaluative sort can make no contribution to effective teaching. Its function is rather to select pupils, gradually as they pass through our schools, for different positions in the socio-economic hierarchy of our society, positions for which we then proceed to train them. Thus the way in which we use examinations and other assessment techniques suggests that we attach much greater importance to this goal of social selection than to the quality of our teaching.

But is it not overstating the case to suggest that giving pupils marks does not help in teaching them? Surely they provide the basis for grouping pupils into appropriate sets or classes for teaching? The case against ability grouping is made elsewhere in this book (see pp. 142–50), but the relevant point for the present argument is that the case *for* ability grouping rests upon the supposed advantages of teaching *similar* pupils together. The trouble with assessing pupils in terms of marks is that it is a procedure which conceals and distorts the similarities and differences between pupils.

In giving pupils marks for, say, English, we are pretending to measure something called 'English attainment'. The measurement of human personality characteristics is quite a feasible, though difficult, operation. But to translate responses to the various tasks set in a school examination into numbers is not measurement, for measurement is only possible when one has defined a dimension, like length or time, with regard to which things can only differ by being more or less than one another. In contrast, a pupil with 50 per cent in an English exam will often have been given more marks on some parts of the paper, the literature questions perhaps, than another with 60 per cent; and there may be nothing in common between the responses of two pupils each given 50 per cent. 'English attainment', as defined in terms of a school exam, is like physical health – people do not simply have more or less of it; different marks represent a meaningless sort of amalgam of the many types of qualitative differences between pupils.

This elaborate pseudo-measurement is unfortunately not just useless from the teaching point of view, it is harmful. For one thing, the time and effort which teachers spend on allocating marks to different responses and on totalling these marks to obtain a final score distracts their attention from the important qualitative characteristics of pupil performances. It is not unknown for pupils to be given only a mark for their examination, essays or exercise, without any information or comments about their strengths and weaknesses. Only rarely do teachers appear to keep records of anything but marks, or to pass any information about pupils except these numbers on to a class's next teacher. Thus teachers rob themselves and their pupils of valuable information, without which neither teaching nor learning can improve as might otherwise be possible.

Moreover, the awarding of marks has a direct negative influence upon the learning of those pupils who do not generally receive high marks. To give a pupil marks of 40 per cent is to attach to him the label of 'low attainer', and because of the influence of this label on the behaviour of teachers, parents and the pupil himself, the chances of subsequent improvement are considerably decreased. Furthermore, it has been found that 'below average' pupils are usually given even lower marks than they expect; and that this, too, has a negative influence upon their attainments, presumably because it discourages them from further effort.

Interpreting examination performances in terms of marks may be unscientific and harmful, but is there any viable alternative? In general conception, at least, this presents no problems. Even at present, *before* attaching marks to pupils' responses we assess them in qualitative terms. A teacher awarding fifteen out of twenty-five to an essay, for example, arrives at this mark by more or less consciously identifying its strengths and weaknesses. The first requirement of an alternative approach is that these qualitative judgements be made explicit. The second requirement is that a *diagnostic summary* should be made of all the various specific judgements and bits of information gleaned from a pupil's paper. Thus the 'result' of a pupil's mathematics exam, *instead of* 40 per cent, might be: 'Has mastered ideas of variable and one-to-one correspondence: not yet clear about functions; gets confused with problems of proportion; still has difficulty in structuring verbal problems (lack of grammatical understanding?); geometry generally competent, but has not learned terminology adequately; considerable skill in analysing visual patterns.' The terms in which such summaries are made must vary with the content and objectives of the teaching which has preceded the examination. Their value will depend on teachers' ability to formulate their own objectives, their understanding of the difficulties which pupils are most likely to have experienced and the appropriateness of the examinations they set.

One context in which a change from pseudo-quantitative to diagnostic assessment is most obviously required is in the training of teachers. The task of teaching depends on so many different social and intellectual skills that it cannot possibly mean much to say that someone is an 'A' or a 'C' teacher; and an extensive body of research supports this conclusion. Furthermore, as many students and supervisors have reported, the requirement that teaching practice supervisors grade their students greatly diminishes the chance of them being effective in their primary role as tutors. Yet these overall ratings of 'teaching ability' are quite pointless except for the purpose of excluding a tiny minority of people from the teaching profession. On the other hand, tutors trained in systematic classroom observation techniques can describe a student's teaching, and diagnose his strengths and weaknesses, with greater reliability than they can attain in making overall ratings. Such diagnostic assessment helps a tutor to focus his attention upon those aspects of teaching in which a student most needs advice or concentrated practice; it helps him to bring the student to a greater awareness of those personal attributes and skills upon which he can most capitalize as a teacher; and, in extreme cases, it helps him to lead a student to perceive for himself that the role of classroom teacher is not one suited to his personality. Here, as in other parts of the educational system, pseudo-measurement is both futile and damaging; and in contrast, fuller and more systematic qualitative assessment could add considerably to the effectiveness of teaching. Perhaps most important, it is through seeing how diagnostic assessment is used in their training, and through experiencing the benefits of it, that young teachers may be encouraged to develop similar procedures in their own teaching.

Finally, let us see the matter in perspective. The present emphasis on grading pupils in terms of marks is very sensible if we are more concerned to sort people into different social strata with an appearance of objectivity than we are with the quality of the teaching our children receive. And for the education system to abandon its function as an agency of social selection (e.g. in determining which pupils should gain the socio-economic rewards attached to a university education) would imply fundamental changes in the structure of society. So, while the quality of assessment in teaching is dependent on complex professional skills, the *sort* of assessment we want is dependent on a political choice: more effective teaching or helping to maintain the hierarchical nature of society. The shift towards comprehensive patterns of education has made the grading of pupils less 'necessary'; by using this opportunity to abandon grading procedures, headmasters and teachers can help both to make these organizational changes fruitful and also to extend them.

# Part Five
**Tertiary**

# Nanette Whitbread
## The Education of Teachers

Nanette Whitbread has taught in secondary modern
and comprehensive schools, including one year in
Canada. She has been senior lecturer in education for
the past six years at the Leicester College of Education.
She is an assistant editor of the educational journal
'Forum' and a member of the editorial board of 'Education
for Teaching'. She is a member of the executive of
the Association of Teachers in Colleges and Departments
of Education.

Any conflicts of purpose within the education system can be
expected to exert pressures on and within the colleges where
teachers are trained, and these conflicts themselves reflect the
contradictory pressures in the structure of contemporary society.
It is worth examining some of the resulting tensions within the
education of teachers and the contribution that colleges of
education can make to the development of democracy.

Every inquiry from the Cross Commission in 1888 to the last
report of the National Advisory Council on the Training and
Supply of Teachers, in 1963, has stressed the urgent need for
more and better qualified teachers. In *Society and the Education
of Teachers* (1969), William Taylor showed that nearly half the
men and over a third of the women students now come from the
manual working class and 'that the colleges of education are
drawing upon educationally inferior groups as compared with
the university' measured in terms of A-level qualifications (admittedly of dubious prognostic value). The colleges occupy an
ambiguous position in the educational and social hierarchy as a
relatively privileged preserve, yet serving the less privileged
sectors of the school system. Herein lies a source of conflict
within the culture of teacher education.

The institutional organization of teacher education has always reflected the class stratification of our society for it has evolved to meet the requirements of a school system which reflects that stratification. Universities have provided teachers for private and grammar schools, while training colleges have served the schools of the working class. Currently these distinctions are beginning to blur as a small proportion of college students take a B.Ed. degree and as secondary schools begin to be reorganized as comprehensives; but the latter development is still very partial and excludes the private and direct-grant sectors, while the B.Ed. remains a degree on the cheap within the binary system. For, contrary to the Robbins Committee's recommendation that colleges of education should be federated in university schools of education, the government decided to leave the colleges under the financial and administrative control of L E As. Writing in *Forum* (spring 1966), Francis Cammaerts rightly forecast that the binary system would 'perpetuate inferior staff–student ratios, inferior salaries of teachers, inferior provision of libraries and equipment and inferior conditions for students' in colleges of education and the rest of the local authority sector of higher education. Until there is a unitary system of higher education, with a unitary system of teacher education within it, this will remain true and the quality of education for the majority of teachers will be impoverished.

Government vacillation and a stop–go policy towards expansion of the colleges of education has reflected the struggle between democracy and elitism, in which the latter has been aided by pressure to restrict public spending in a predominantly private, capitalist economy. Continuously increased expansion far into the 1980s, and well in excess of the Robbins estimates, would be needed to eliminate oversized classes, raise the school leaving age as promised under section 35 of the 1944 Education Act, permit nation-wide provision of nursery education, and facilitate regular secondment of teachers for in-service courses; failure on each of these issues hits at the educational opportunity of large numbers of working-class children. Successive governments have been guilty of anti-democratic mismanagement of teacher supply. This has resulted in a five-year period of expansion without capital expenditure, when students and staff in colleges of education suffered a worsening in working conditions through severe overcrowding and the operation of 'Box and Cox' shift systems. Such problems, together with the binary tangle, hinder attempts to introduce an in-service B.Ed., which is urgently needed as a democratic and professional right to speed the transition to a graduate profession.

These problems are partly responsible for the colleges' failure to undertake any radical reappraisal of their courses following the introduction of the three-year course in 1960 and the B.Ed. in 1966. Consequently they have contributed little to curriculum innovation in the schools or to educational research. There has been a kind of paralysis in colleges of education. It stems from an inability to resolve conflicts inherent in their role as agents for conformity or change, social cohesion or cultural revolution. They are placed in an ideological dilemma on which they avoid fundamental commitment. Because of ambiguity in their own status, some college of education tutors prefer to ignore issues of social class and direct social criticism to less directly political matters, such as pop culture and the ethics of the mass media.

In *The Experience of Higher Education* (1964), Peter Marris described how university and technical college students were hostile to the concept of social class. This hostility is even greater in colleges of education where William Taylor has reported (in *Society and the Education of Teachers*): '. . . there is still the feeling on the part of some tutors, as well as students, that the topic is "embarrassing" and best avoided'. Because students may be in the process of moving from their parental class to that of their future career, and are hence between classes, they are often confused and ambivalent.

A feature of the ideological dilemma is that the colleges are functionally committed to promoting upward social mobility among their own students and to raising working-class educational standards in the schools; but they are simultaneously expected to be agents of social cohesion, to condition students to identify themselves as future teachers with a middle-class profession and to accept the *status quo* of our class society as reflected in the schools. The majority of students find it easier not to face up to this contradiction, but to concentrate on the acquisition of teaching skills and the narrowly vocational aspects of training. Tutors prefer to propagate a child-centered attitude and a missionary approach to the education of the under-privileged.

But there are signs of a groping towards more explicit commitment among both students and staff. Student radicals, despite the lack of analysis in *Student Power* (Cockburn and Blackburn, 1969) and other writings, have recognized important features of education and the bourgeois state. The 1969 conference of students in colleges of education demanded a government inquiry into their training, and this was supported by the Association of Teachers in Colleges and Departments of Education. At the first national conference of new college lecturers, an articulate minority was anxious to probe the ideological issues in teacher education, and there was evidence of general readiness for radical reappraisal of the whole college course.

The James Committee was set up late in 1970 to investigate and make recommendations on teacher education at a time when staff and students were ready for reform. It was required to carry out this important task within about one year, and to take into account the reviews already being undertaken by each Area Training Organization at the request of the previous Secretary of State and the published Report by the House of Commons Select Committee on Education and Science (1969) on 'Student Relations'. As Tyrrell Burgess has pointed out in his Introduction to *Dear Lord James* (1971), the terms of reference of this first inquiry into teacher education since the McNair Report in 1944 are too limited. Radical reappraisal can result only if the Committee reviews teacher education in the context of the evolution of a democratic structure of higher education consequent upon comprehensive secondary education, new trends in the schools and the role of teachers in a democratic society.

The colleges are becoming committed to non-streaming in schools, to comprehensive secondary education and, at least in part, to the concept of mass educability. Resenting inferior status as monotechnics serving an undervalued profession, they published a policy statement in 1970 and submitted evidence through their professional organization (Association of Teachers in Colleges and Departments of Education) to the James Committee in 1971 showing that they seek to enlarge their function and so share in expansion of higher education. The growing resentment among students at early captive commitment to one career, through a Certificate that is valueless for anything but teaching, has encouraged this policy as the ATCDE recognized that monotechnics will fail to attract able sixth formers. Generally opposed to elitism in education, the colleges are becoming identified with pressures for a democratic structure of education at all levels, including a more rational and unified pattern of tertiary. But few of their members are yet politically committed to the social change implicit in these educational reforms.

Courses for the Teacher's Certificate have been modified and added to but not many have been radically restructured for many decades. Reform has been impeded by difficulty in reconciling academic and professional claims on the content and balance of courses. The colleges must pursue a professional objective, accepting the utilitarian criterion of the relevance of knowledge for intending teachers while resisting pressure for a return to an ethos of apprenticeship. They should heed the criticism in the report approved by the 1969 National Young Teachers' Conference that they do not prepare students to contribute to important new developments such as non-streaming, team teaching and curriculum reform. Colleges cannot do this by reliance on developing diffuse vocational commitment through a romantic, child-centered course alongside unrelated study of traditional academic subjects. A rational, intellectually demanding and more coherent approach is required to the study of both the subjects students will teach and of the disciplines of educational psychology, sociology, history and philosophy. As the report recognized, 'all areas of professional education should be equally rigorous intellectually'. Teaching practice could then develop judgement and expertise.

A more rigorously intellectual approach to teacher education will help students and tutors to become more rational teachers, better able to meet demands to evaluate innovation in the schools and colleges, and to make reasoned rather than intuitive decisions. By initiating college students more effectively into the world of rational intellect it will be offering them a higher education worthy of the name.

This is asking a lot of a three-year concurrent or one-year postgraduate course which must include an adequate amount of practical teaching. If the mass of the population are to have teachers sufficiently qualified to meet present-day demands, a four-year graduate course must become the minimum qualification. The different emphases in the requirements of primary, middle-school, secondary and sixth-form teachers necessitate considerable variations in their initial course – concurrent, consecutive, range of professional courses, extent of subject specialization, etc. The authors of *Dear Lord James* (1971), exploring many of the inherent problems in some detail, forcibly argued the need for more demanding courses differentiated according to these requirements, an end to the isolation of teacher education and for systematic expansion of in-service education. Following the demise of the monotechnic and teenage commitment to teaching, initial courses for future teachers will have to dovetail with professional courses for other careers and new types of degree. This will require flexibility and ingenuity; but such complex patterns will be necessary to a unitary system of higher education in which graduate teacher education and a coherent pattern for further in-service qualifications form a significant part.

These are all issues which the James Committee should consider. To be of any value their report, expected early in 1972, will therefore need to be radical. It could provide the impetus not only for reform of the structure and content of courses leading to graduate qualifications for all teachers, but also for enabling the colleges to become the spearpoint of innovation in a system of higher education designed to serve a democratic society. A democracy must attract able people to the teaching profession. To do so it must establish teacher education uncompromisingly within higher education and, as Peter Venables has pointed out (in *Patterns and Policies in Higher Education*, Brosan, *et al.* (1971)) cease to display 'a curious lack of confidence in the normal methods of securing sufficient recruits for a profession'. The James Committee must cause government and public to recognize the financial corollaries, in terms of recruitment to the profession and widened functions of the colleges, of worthwhile recommendations on the education of teachers.

Reform of the content of courses cannot alone provide the necessary intellectual discipline and independence. Lectures and tutor-dominated discussions should largely give place to methods of teaching that involve more active participation and self-programming by students, and transfer the onus for learning to them. This is the object of some of the newer teaching methods now in use.

Syndicate work by small groups of students on planned assignments, as described by K. G. Collier in *New Dimensions in Higher Education* (1968), demands more independent thought, induces greater student involvement in the work and promotes intellectual stimulus. In my experience such a method, whereby groups of students are asked to investigate a problem and apportion aspects among themselves, also improves students' ability to programme their own individual assignments and encourages a self-directed approach to learning. Task-directed free group discussion without the tutor, as described by M. L. J. Abercrombie in *The Anatomy of Judgment* (1960), helps students to make better judgements, to distinguish between evidence and inference and to improve oral verbalization. These methods have much in common with the problem solving, learning by discovery and group work now used in schools; subjective experience and subsequent discussion of similar ways of learning at their own level should give students greater insight into the processes, and hence enable them to use these means more effectively with children. Ruth Beard's *Teaching and Learning in Higher Education* (1970) should help tutors to determine their objectives and devise appropriate methods to use with their students.

Non-didactic methods automatically invoke student participation in course planning and alter the traditional relationship between tutors and students. This is the academic aspect of student representation and participation in the running of colleges in a democratic society. Student participation is particularly viable in colleges of education where the students are presumptive members of the same profession as their tutors and where both are committed to the improvement of the whole education system. The Education (No. 2) Act 1968, in force from July 1969, secures some staff and student participation in

the running of their colleges and hence provides for a further
dimension in teacher education. Ordinary teachers need to be
prepared for taking part in the process of discussion and planning
that must precede effective innovation in the curriculum and in
democratizing the traditional authority structure in schools.
This is more urgent now that the N U T has set up a Working
Party on teacher participation which will report to the 1972
conference.

When a college of education student, Anthony Padfield,
analysed student expectations in the *Teacher* (23 May 1969),
he included 'the right to influence, participate in and exercise
control over decisions affecting their own lives and work'.
These are the legitimate rights to be expected in a participatory
democracy, but they are rights which can be exercised responsibly and effectively only if people learn the appropriate skills
by practising them in a microcosm; educational institutions,
particularly those of higher education, provide those micro-
cosms and are failing in part of their democratic and educational
purpose if they do not facilitate this function. For colleges of
education this role is a part of their contribution to that cultural
revolution which is essential to the development of democracy.

# Les Brook
## Further What?

Les Brook taught in a primary school before reading
politics at University College, Swansea, where he was
Union President and Chairman of the Welsh NUS.
After two years' further education teaching in Worthing,
he spent a year qualifying for the Cert. Ed. at Garnett
College of Education (Technical). He is on the ATTI
Education Committee and edits 'Further Left', a
socialist magazine for teachers in further and higher
education.

When, in December 1970, a teacher told the delegates to the
National Education Conference that a time-clock had been
installed in an East Lancashire college, reaction was strong.
Shock, disquiet, outrage were in evidence. And yet it would
have been more consistent for the majority of the assembled
lecturers to have met this revelation with a round of applause.
Further education has always been as much an appendage of the
factory as part of the educational system. Nowhere in that
system can there be a sector with so many commercial and
industrial links. The presence of employers on governing bodies
is institutionalized in the Instruments of Government of the
colleges. Curricula are devised to meet the needs of industry and
commerce. Teachers entering further education are expected to
have had industrial experience, and are encouraged to act as
consultants to large firms. Departments are closed because
industries contract. The majority of the students – those on
day-release and sandwich courses, as well as many studying at
evening classes – are employees, even when at college.

All of this is open and carried on without apology. Thus it is
that when a day-release gas fitter arrives late for his 9.00 lecture
at the local tech., the teacher not only notes his lateness and

rebukes him for it, but also, at 10.00 when the class finishes, completes a postcard to be sent to his employer:

---

Dear *Mr Brown*

Your employee, *A White*
was late for/~~was absent from~~ the following
classes on *25 September 1971 – Mathematics*


Yours faithfully *S Black*
Head of Science and Engineering Dept

---

The installation of a time-clock for employees on day-release considerably eases the problem for both staff and students. It represents a definite advance in organizational efficiency. And since most further education teachers believe it correct that the employer should be informed, and indeed should discipline those who abuse the 'privilege' of day-release, then to be outraged by the installation is sheer hypocrisy.

The development of technical education is the story of the recognition by British industry that international competition demands a trained, domestic labour force. Whilst most historians trace the origins of the present system back to the Mechanics Institute of the nineteenth century, further education (a significant change in title, it will be noted) is essentially a post-Second World War phenomenon. Even where it is argued that the tenfold increase in full-time students in further education between the beginning of the century and 1938 is greater than the fourfold increase since the war, it has to be conceded that absolute growth since the war has dwarfed that before, and that the structure of further education nowadays has little or nothing to do with that of the pre-war period. Further, the whole emphasis has changed as the proportion of the student population who are on full-time and advanced courses has dramatically increased. Not only has part-time education shown a relative decline; its emphasis has also changed from vocational evening work to part-time day release and sandwich courses.

The 1956 White Paper *Technical Education* rationalized and restructured further education for the era of the giant companies, nationalized industries and intensified international competition. It was preceded by a speech by Winston Churchill in which he drew attention to Russian advances in technology and technical education. The White Paper made no bones about it;

From the USA, Russia and Western Europe comes the challenge to look to our system of technical education. . . . The aims are to strengthen the foundations of our economy, to improve the standards of living of our people, and to discharge effectively our manifold responsibilities overseas.

The structure of technical education was to parallel more closely the structure of industry; students were to be matched to identifiable technical processes. Thus three categories of trainees were identified: the technologist, the technician and the craftsman. Courses and qualifications were to be geared to this structure. Colleges were to be designated 'Regional', 'Area' or 'Local' according to the level of their courses. Growth has since been justified by, and has taken place within this hierarchy. As the Henniker-Heaton Report *Day Release* put it in 1964.

The education of all young people must keep in step so that the necessary support is given to the increasing numbers who will qualify for the technological and managerial posts.

The character of this structure has been largely masked by the changing character of vocational education. Even the White Paper spoke of technical education not being too narrowly vocational; 'Swift change is the characteristic of our age, so that a main purpose of the technical education of the future must be to teach boys and girls to be adaptable.' In the local and area colleges, there has been an 132·3 per cent rise in the amount of ostensibly non-vocational A-level GCE work between 1961 and 1969. In the regional colleges, ostensibly non-vocational degree work has increased at an even more alarming rate. Large dollops of liberal studies have been grafted on to courses for craftsmen, supposedly making them instantly less objectionable. Despite such diversions, much of the work now being most rapidly developed in the further education sector is quite obviously and openly geared to industrial and commercial needs. The CNAA degrees in the polytechnics have a solid vocational content, and the ONDs in the local and area colleges (showing a rise of no less than 340 per cent since 1961) are at once both general and vocational qualifications. But the most important step towards total accommodation to the needs of industry has been the 1964 Industrial Training Act which reformed a much-maligned apprenticeship system by creating a number of Industrial Training Boards, dominated by 'industry', to improve and increase training. Whilst totally failing to increase the further education chances of the young worker, it has meant that industrial control of yet another section of further education has increased.

The economic orientation of further education has, para-doxically, been the cause of its growth and also the reason it has failed to realize its full potential, both in terms of the numbers of students involved and the quality of their education. Inside the colleges, reporting to employers on what Henniker–Heaton called 'routine disciplinary matters of punctuality, attendance and behaviour' is only one aspect of external control. The standards enforced by college authorities are often those of the most reactionary of employers, or those held by employers when the lecturers were themselves employees. Minis, maxis and hot pants have all been forbidden to full-time secretarial students because they would not be acceptable to employers. Academic freedom is inevitably at a premium. Apart from external control of the curriculum by the moguls of the City and Guilds of London Institute, the Royal Society of Arts, the GCE boards, London University and the Industrial Training Boards, inter-ference can be just as crude as the departmental head who told the sociology teacher that he should have started a lesson on industrial relations with the 'small group of politically-motivated men' theory. When told that this view was to be dealt with in lecture two of the series, he remarked that some of the students may not come to that one! But the problem is often sharpest for those who have a nominal freedom to draw up their own syl-labuses. On a proposal to run a liberal studies life-saving course for boat-builder apprentices, a departmental head told me he didn't think he could justify it to the employers. One can draw one's own conclusions about the consequences of more con-troversial proposals.

It will be clear that the process of economic interference and control seldom operates in an open and personal manner, but through a hierarchy of reactionary authority stretching from government departments through local authorities and into the colleges themselves. Principals and heads of departments, as well as being largely reactionary as a body, over-react to situations in much the same way as other bureaucratic administrators. They receive support from many teachers who subscribe to a more or less elaborate ideology which serves to justify and perpetuate the *status quo*. It goes like this: the education system's primary function is the maintenance and promotion of the existing social system. This system depends for its continued existence on a developing economic position. The function of further education is to train the necessary manpower. A related pedagogic ideology is propounded – 'the student appreciates that the college work is real, that it is important and that it has a value that is apparent in terms of material advancement and social prestige' (A T T I policy statement). The economic function of the college is thus complemented by the vocational orientation of the student. And there is no need, given that we live in a rapidly changing society with a dynamic economy, for such an ideology to be illiberal. To quote the A T T I once more

The changes that take place in our society need, and will continue to need, a better and more extensive pattern of education than we provide today. The changes in technology and the increases in automation are leading to a demand for better educated people at all levels. This will make new calls on the education system which will have to prepare young people who are well educated and capable of adapting themselves rapidly to new situations, new techniques, new jobs. It will involve giving both more general and more vocational education.

For all this, the liberal approach does not co-exist easily with the economic justification. The fact is that if a further education system is primarily committed to matching college courses to known manpower needs, it will succeed in training only those whose productivity can be significantly increased by such training. Conversely, it will be unable to justify any form of training or education for the unskilled, or even the semi-skilled, worker. The 1956 White Paper did not even include a category for such people, and when the Crowther Report proposed a new 'operative' category in 1959, the unskilled and many of the semi-skilled were not included. In November 1969 only 40 per cent of insured boys under eighteen and 10 per cent of girls were released by their employers to take part in day-release courses. Altogether, nearly a million eligible sixteen to eighteen year olds were completely outside the education system (figures calculated from *Statistics of Education*, 1969). With very rare exceptions, colleges have failed to offer courses for the semi-skilled and unskilled young worker, and even fewer have made a success of them. Of course, 'There's no demand for such courses.' Should anybody wonder?

True to its ideology and economic demands, the major developments in further education in the last few years have been in higher level work. Following the hiving-off of the colleges of advanced technology by the Tories, Labour began, in 1966, to hive-off much of the degree level work being undertaken in the regional colleges. The polytechnics have been evolved to cater, at low cost, for the production of highly trained, specialized manpower. Whilst the 'education-on-the-cheap' bit is vehemently denied in the teeth of the facts, the polys' vocational orientation has been openly accepted as public policy. If one were generous, one might believe that behind the establishment of the polys was a genuine desire to create a comprehensive system of further and higher education, a system of people's universities, sustained by and sustaining urban and largely working-class communities, and bringing together both the trainee manager and the tea boy in an educational collective. But even if one were so generous, one would have to express alarm at the naïvete of those who believe that St Poly can take on, and, after a period of fair combat, defeat, the University dragon. For the universities are as much a part of that hierarchy of institutions, whose primary purpose is to meet the demands of the economy, as are the polys. And surely we have learnt from the experience of the tripartite division of secondary education and the CATs that educational institutions in a class society are not independent but perform definite social functions?

Thus, like the CATs before them, the polys, far from competing with the universities, are caught up in the scramble to become universities. Far from developing as comprehensive institutions, many are busy shelling off the lower-level, lower-class and lower-paid work. Their courses are torn between the vocational, liberal orientation which the economy demands, and the academic orientation which the institutional hierarchy favours. They scamper after research whilst teaching standards leave much to be desired. They look to the universities where middle-class boys and girls learn what middle-class boys and girls should learn, and turn their backs on the GPO boys, the basic apprentices, and the plumbers.

Despite its total inadequacy, the polytechnic ideal remains one of the few visions of recent further education thinking. The urgent need is to construct a new vision of what further education should be all about, a vision which aims at a decisive break between institutions, students and curricula on the one hand, and economic demand on the other. The philosophy underlying this vision must be student-centred, and the student must be seen not merely as a potential worker but as a potential adult human being. Similarly, work must be seen as part of life, and not as life itself. Further education will continue to have responsibility for work education, but must interpret this responsibility in terms of the fulfilment of the student rather than that of an impersonal system. In relation to work, as in relation to life as a whole, education must be seen as a process of increasing the student's capacity to control his own environment.

The programme based upon such an approach will have as its first aim to draw all under-eighteens into the further-education system. It is imperative that the ability of the economy to determine the education of this age group be drastically curtailed. Work experience, if any, would be on the basis of release from college under the guidance of teachers. The colleges themselves must be comprehensive, embracing all young people whatever their aims or interests. Only by the creation of genuinely comprehensive tertiary colleges can success be achieved in abolishing the hierarchical distinctions which riddle the present system and in presenting the student with a broad spectrum of life, and work, possibilities.

The colleges themselves must be democratically organized communities, breaking the present economic grip on college life, and primarily on curriculum development. The burden of educating these young people must be placed squarely on the

shoulders of the teachers, although the help which can be given
by enlightened agencies for curriculum innovation (such as we
have in the primary schools) cannot be overestimated. The
students themselves must be totally involved in building this
community, and primarily in helping their teachers to develop
relevant and stimulating courses. Democratization of the colleges
is the first step to tearing down the tyranny of external examinations, the chief instrument in the categorization of the student
as a particular type of economic animal.

In higher education, the binary system must be destroyed as
part of a programme to establish comprehensive polyversities.
But, as in the tertiary colleges, structural change must be accompanied by democratic advance in the organization of these
institutions, and curriculum innovation on a massive scale. Just
as in the comprehensive school the old tripartite pattern can
remain under the guise of streaming, so in the polyversity and
tertiary college, we cannot be satisfied until new courses, geared
to student needs, are presented by teachers who cannot rely on
external pressures to motivate the student, but who feel *themselves* totally responsible for the student's progress in thinking
and learning.

The demand for 'More!' in present circumstances can never
be a truly progressive battle-cry. There is, after all, going to be
more, whether we like it or not. Even so, we must be asking for
increases in educational spending but without illusions that some
mysterious dialectical process will create qualitative from
quantitative changes. Alongside such demands, progressives in
further and higher education must be developing an alternative
philosophy and an alternative programme for educational advance. The demand must then be for the implementation of that
programme. The logical extension of 'More!' is 'Education for
all!' When we have got the 'education' bit right, then 'More!'
becomes a truly revolutionary demand.

# Alistair Kee
## Demystifying the University

Alistair Kee lectures in Theology at the University of
Hull. He studied at Glasgow University before taking his
doctor's degree at Union Theological Seminary, New
York. From 1965 to 1967 he taught at the University
College of Rhodesia. His writings on the social and
political implications of education include 'Students at
Hull' (1968). He has recently published 'The Way of
Transcendence' (1971) and is currently Chairman of the
Lecturing and Administrative Staff Association at Hull.

There is a mystique surrounding the university, and to a lesser
extent those connected with it. The majority of people in the
land maintain the university but understand nothing about it. It
purports to have developed standards of its own by which all
but a few people are failures. It confers status on its own, and
shuns investigation from outside. So long as the mystique is
allowed to persist we shall not know whether the university's
standards are reputable and whether its relations with society are
justifiable. And I suspect that education itself will continue to
suffer until demystification has taken place.

### The institution

The mystique surrounding the university has prevented any
depth analysis of the university's nature and purpose from
within. The university has a certain ethos, and it has been
unthinkingly assumed that the institution can be perpetuated
from generation to generation by its own successful students,
provided they have absorbed the ethos. The nature and purpose
of the university? One of the most depressing features of the
period of unrest within the universities was the exposure of the
fact that the senior academics and administrators, who had as

they said, 'committed their lives' to the university, had really given no thought to its nature and purpose. They fell back on the ethos approach, even an aesthetic approach: a university is a university is a university. Some analogies were inept, though very revealing: the university is like a hospital. This from a national figure who had given his life to the university. How did he complete his census form on the nature of his employment and the purpose of the institution in which he worked? In practice they no doubt thought of the university on the model of some kind of school in which the young and ignorant learn from the mature and learned. And yet the lie was given to this approach when the mature and learned were unable to give an answer to the first question: what is the nature and purpose of the university? The crisis in confidence, leadership and authority in the university stems from the fact that when the stokers and black squad of the good ship *Universitas* finally asked where it was heading for, it was discovered that, notwithstanding an impressive amount of fiddling with knobs and shouting of orders, no one on the bridge had actually plotted a course. The mystique, it appears, is all that is required. Calm again has been restored. Time, if it does not produce answers, at least gets rid of awkward questioners, and the generation of students of 1968 have been safely seen off, leaving the top brass not to find real answers to these fundamental questions, but to return gladly to their routine fiddling and shouting. Still no plotting of a course, let alone a new and purposeful one.

This is an age of massive public spending and therefore an age of public accountability. Yet because of the mystique surrounding the university the institution has so far fended off any investigation of its workings. Academic standards, academic freedom! These are the slogans of the mystique, as if academics were not men of flesh and blood, as susceptible as other mortals to prejudice, self-interest and anti-social activities. The impact of the university on society is such that academic responsibility cannot now be justified independent of social criteria. Government spending is such that academic standards must be linked to economic priorities through the country. There are fashions in medical research. By what social criteria are they measured when academic freedom is exercised? Yet the university is allowed to run its own affairs largely without interference from outside.

Every area of society is the responsibility of a government department. Yet such is the mystique of the university that the Department of Education and Science did not intervene in 1968 when one university after another was disrupted. If public money were wasted and the life of the nation threatened by a breakdown in the hospital system, then the Secretary for Health and Social Security would be remiss not to intervene. Indeed his department should have been sufficiently in touch to prevent things getting to the break point. Similarly the Secretary for Trade and Industry must be accountable especially when public money or the national economy is at risk and a dispute could have been prevented. And yet the university seems to be beyond the competence of successive Secretaries for Education and Science to understand or influence. It was therefore quite fascinating to read in November 1968 that Parliament decided to set up a Select Committee to look into the matter. The wording of the Order was, 'That a Select Committee be appointed to consider the activities of the Department of Education and Science and the Scottish Education Department and to report thereon this Session.' Here at last was a Select Committee which would ask why it was that such an important institution had been allowed to get into such a mess. But it would have been quite naïve to imagine that the Select Committee would do what it was actually set up to do. The Committee immediately changed its name, significantly, to 'The Select Committee on Education and Science', and changed its remit to investigating student unrest. Its report was entitled, *Student Relations*, and accepted in July 1969 by Parliament, although it had nothing at all to do with the Order or the remit under which it was set up. Why was this? Simply because it could not be imagined that there could be anything wrong with the university itself. Drawing from our recent history we know that when the natives were restless it meant there was something wrong with the natives. It could never be that there was something wrong with the colonial administrators whose word was law. A government department never needed to investigate administrations. On the apparently unquestionable assumption that the university unrest stemmed from *student* problems, the Select Committee decided it would be nicer to investigate students than the university itself, much nicer than investigating the Department of Education and Science. Not that the Select Committee failed to visit universities and speak to staff and students, or even as they called them, 'the authorities'. The Committee or its subcommittees visited twelve universities in England and Wales, and four in Scotland. The chairmen of the subcommittees even went to Paris for a few days. But neither in the evidence of the hearings nor in the report of the Committee was the mystique of the university penetrated. The recommendations could have been (perhaps were) written in advance, and concern the running of the ship and the delegation of duties. Still no question about plotting a course. It was ironic, though predictable, that the politicians who made up the Select Committee refused to take seriously the political dimensions of student unrest. Even the historical section of *Student Relations* was researched for them by *Reader's Digest*.

The storm was weathered, and peace has been restored, or at least apathy now rules. The mystique has been preserved, but the institution is the poorer for it, certainly for the way in which the *status quo* has been preserved. It is poorer because it has not faced up to the questions about its nature and purpose, its role in society, its responsibility to its own society and to the rest of the world, not least the Two-Thirds World. But the institution is also the poorer for further alienating its own students. What could be more ironic than an institution nominally committed to encouraging and stimulating inquiring minds, angrily cutting off any debate about the institution itself – angrily because the questions were cogent and the answers not forthcoming. Little wonder that students are apathetic about participation in the running of such a closed system.

## The students

If the university authorities are existentially committed to maintaining the mystique of the university, and political leaders are unwilling to penetrate it, it is quite possible that demystification will take place from within by successive generations of students. The age of majority has been lowered to eighteen. This has not achieved anything: it simply gives legal recognition to a fact that could no longer be ignored, namely that since the 1940s the level of consciousness among minors has been sharply raised. This means that students enter the university now as citizens, as adults and not as overgrown schoolchildren. I want to take this point up again in a moment, but there is another aspect of the youth scene which is not generally recognized. Teenage tastes and activities now belong to the eleven to fourteen-year-old group. By comparison students, even at eighteen, are part of the adult generation. During their university years they are deciding which adult society to join, the straight or the alternative. But contrary to the romantic view of the institution, they do not join the university, for it is not a society. It is a phenomenon within straight society, and yet it is not openly and honestly related to that society. As the level of consciousness is raised, students, whether for the straight or the alternative options, are beginning to see through the university, and are asking *it* to grow up. They are refusing to take seriously the mystique of authority and status which have nothing to do with education. Demystification has begun, and that is another factor in the rather cool attitude the students now have to the university.

But if students are to demystify the university, then to be consistent they must demystify the image of the student, particularly outside the university. The first area in which this should be done concerns the relationship of students to society. This is made difficult not only by the current spread of students through the country through the UCCA scheme, but also because on reaching the university they find that invariably it has been allowed to develop as an alien institution within its town or city. Physically the institution is alien to the local population. They dare not stray onto the campus to see what it is about, and the residential halls seem like private hotels for another kind of being. Spiritually the institution is alien. The local people – of course – could have no interest in questions of life, judgement, value. Students can contribute to the demystification of the university by insisting that their primary allegiance is to society and not to an alien and alienating institution.

Another essential change in the role of the student must be the loss of their present status *vis-à-vis* the law. This may seem an odd point to make at a time when the media have been saturated with coverage of students fighting the police. Precisely. How do we know that they are students? And if some of them are, so what? As long as students have a special image as an immature lot, somewhere between school and a job, then they do a disservice to the causes they take up. Too often the media have been able to take the easy way out by using the fact that the demonstrators are students (and we all know what *that* means) to obscure the importance or validity of the issue in dispute. When students have no special position in society the causes may then be furthered more effectively. The other side of the issue is that the university must be considered to be an ordinary part of society, with no special status before the law. There is no need for a warden to try to exercise the housemaster's authority when excessive noise continues at 3.00 a.m. Ordinary citizens know what to do about this. If university property is maliciously damaged, then there must be recourse to the ordinary processes of law. I think it is most important for students that they do not allow the university to protect them from the law, for this is the beginning of a very dangerous road indeed. One of the more recent turnings on this road is the necessity then for the university to build up its own files on its students, and even build up its own private security force. There is growing concern about secret files gradually being built up throughout society as a whole. Black lists (for example with regard to credit rating) once made are taken seriously no matter the quality of the evidence in their compilation. We certainly do not need a black list of students and staff circulating from university to government or industry.

If students are able to demystify their own role between society and the university then the attitudes of certain L E As must change. There is no doubt that some L E As enjoy exercising their power and control over the students who happen to come from their areas. Students have always encountered people only too willing to exercise the negative aspects of parental control. As the head of the boarding school writes to give a report on the child's progress, the university gives a report to the L E A. There is no objection to a simple report, that the student has satisfied the university's academic requirements for the year. What is quite intolerable is that some L E As look for – and no doubt receive – reports of a non-academic nature. Since students are now citizens, the provision of grants must be put on a proper legal basis. A mother is not instructed on how a family allowance should be spent. No one tells a man how his unemployment benefit should be used. Nor is it withheld if he has been attending a political rally. It is hoped that adult citizens will use wisely the money to which they are entitled under the law. But it would be intolerable if the state intervened to insist on any kind of pattern and priorities. The L E As must give up their self-appointed role as guardians of the double standard. It is a great opportunity for a young person to get to university, where there was no such possibility in his family before. But the situation today is such that going to university on a state grant cannot be looked upon as a special privilege. Great Britain needs university graduates in order to survive in the modern world. More than North Sea Gas it needs to develop the natural resources of its next generation. More than nuclear submarines it needs to channel the creative power of its young minds. More than a modern army it needs to develop the skills of the new professionals. No matter how much of an opportunity is given to students the state is more than willing to pay them to attend university. Students hold their grants by law and not patronage and should have them withdrawn or threatened only when their legal eligibility comes to an end, i.e. when they leave university successfully or unsuccessfully.

My intention in arguing for the demystification of the university has not been to weaken the institution, but rather to discover how it can be further strengthened and developed. What is its nature and what are its possibilities? How is it related to society and how should it be? Is it the last bastion against the disintegration of society, or is it the greatest obstacle to the creation of a new society? My dismay is not that no answers have been forthcoming to such fundamental questions, but that they are regarded as peripheral to the real job of continuing to do what we have always been doing in roughly the same way. I am not hopeful that the university will take the initiative and destroy its own mystique. My hope lies in the fact that each year, in increasing numbers, the university is flooded with new students.

# Colin Stoneman
# The Purpose of Universities and Colleges – and their Government

**Colin Stoneman has been lecturer in Chemistry at the University of Hull since 1964. He is on the editorial board of the 'Spokesman'.**

### Purpose

It is of course always easier to criticize than it is to construct. The dismantling of unhealthy or outdated structures may be of first importance, but it is even more important to replace them with something superior. Although a detailed blueprint is rarely a good idea, as many details can only be worked out in actual practice, it is important to keep the principles on which one is going to work clearly in mind.

There have always been two main reasons for the existence of colleges and universities. The first, generally emphasized by conservatives, was to train people for the professions, and to provide society with some other services. The second, given more predominance by liberals, was to engage in the pursuit of learning and research for their own sake.

If pure learning is to survive as one of the purposes of a university, it will have to be brought into relation with the life of the community as a whole, not only with the refined delights of a few gentlemen of leisure. I regard disinterested learning as a matter of great importance, and I should wish to see its place in academic life increased, not diminished (Bertrand Russell, *On Education*, 1926).

However, the simple distinction between the purposes of turning out more doctors and lawyers and chemists on the one hand, and investigating the nature of the universe without regard to immediate utility, on the other, cannot now be maintained (if it ever could be). About the time Russell wrote the above, Rutherford, then engaged in research into the atomic nucleus, was proudly proclaiming that his work, although intensely interesting and important for its own sake, was of no conceivable use to mankind. But it is not just a question of being unable to predict the social consequences of one's research: societies are also a part of the universe, and research into their social, economic, political and psychological aspects has grown by leaps and bounds over the last few decades. In part this has been at the request of the Government, to help solve problems through more careful analysis of how society works. Already this brings us on to dangerous ground, for however interesting these matters may be, research into them cannot be disinterested, as the intention is to consolidate the *status quo* rather than to change it. But in part also this interest has been motivated by a dissatisfaction with society: critical analyses have often been made as the admitted first step before proposing radical changes. Clearly this is not disinterested research, but it is *no less* disinterested than research designed to serve society as it happens to be.

So if it is accepted that the pursuit of learning for its own sake is a valid purpose for a university, the conclusion is inescapable that its scholars must be allowed to investigate society, and criticize its contradictions, injustices and inconsistencies. It becomes impossible to make any divorce between the roles of critical scholar and critical citizen. So here we may suggest a third purpose for the university, not easily assimilable into the other two: to act as the conscience of society, helping to preserve what is good in it, and striving to subvert what is bad. A society that is alive to its own long-term interests will license universities to perform this service, accepting the short-term nuisance also created. This was broadly Professor C. B. Macpherson's message when he received an honorary degree in Newfoundland last year:

We must say bluntly that society, and the governments which represent society, are not getting, and cannot get, their money's worth as long as they ask for and expect the wrong product, and that in large measure they are asking for the wrong product . . . the function which society should be asking the university to perform, is dissent: dissent from all the received diagnoses which have failed. That is the only way society can get its money's worth from the university in our days.

He thought that the university could in fact become a modern equivalent of the medieval fool, who alone was licensed to speak the truth to and about the monarch, cutting through the adulation and cant which surrounded him. Just as the sensible prince recognized the value of the fool's service in keeping him from delusions of infallibility, so

a sovereign people stands in as much need of a jester or fool ... [but] a sovereign people, being so numerous, cannot make do with a single jester. It needs a multiple one. And this multiple jester must be made an institution under the protection of the sovereign people. Where else can we find, in a modern society, such a multiple institutionalized jester but in the institution of the university?

A similar theme was developed in a speech in Congress in 1967 by Senator William Fulbright: The universities have failed to form 'an effective counterweight to the military–industrial complex by strengthening their emphasis on the traditional values of our democracy.' Instead they have 'joined the monolith, adding greatly to its power and influence'. Social scientists 'who ought to be acting as responsible and independent critics of the Government's policies' have instead become agents for them. With 'the surrender of independence, the neglect of teaching and the distortion of scholarship' the university 'is not only failing to meet its responsibilities to its students; it is betraying a public trust' (Quoted in Noam Chomsky; *American Power and the New Mandarins*, 1969).

So there are more purposes that a university can, and perhaps should, perform, than is commonly admitted. Exclusive concentration by conservatives on the purpose of supplying society-as-it-is with trained personnel and other services is to recommend the use of the university for narrowly political ends. That some such purpose should be *one* of the purposes (albeit part of a broader purpose concerned with the overall health of society), is not denied. On the other hand, the liberal emphasis on academic freedom

at its worst or most obsolescent smacks of the 'Ivory Tower' ... people outside rarely respect the claim of independence when it is couched in purely negative terms. ... Instead of a negative claim to freedom, we should assert a positive claim to influence. Paradoxically enough, this claim would be a good deal more comprehensible to a wider public outside than the parrot-cry of 'leave us alone - (but pay us more )' (Staff Ad Hoc Group for University Reform (Birmingham University): *No Easy Answers*, 1968).

## Government

There would be no need for democracy in a university whose sole function was to service the *status quo*. Indeed it would be an embarrassment. Of course if the *status quo* were democratic an autocratic university would be anomalous. Plainly also there would be an anomaly in the autocratic rule of an institution solely devoted to freedom of research and disinterested learning. British universities are governed in a uniformly undemocratic manner, a situation which is anomalous in both the above respects. In British society the democratic freedoms are mainly defined negatively, and are narrowly circumscribed so that the contradiction between the national and university modes of government is not too blatant. Some vice-chancellors are even able to claim that their universities are democratic communities (by which they mean that their decisions have to be rubber-stamped by non-elected bodies such as senates or councils). Whatever conflicts there may be between vice-chancellors and the universities' paymasters in society, there can be no doubt that the latter find the former much easier to deal with than they would an elected delegate, responsible to, and reporting back to the whole university community. The more serious anomaly is that between the real measure of academic freedom and the total lack of democratic involvement in government in British universities. The consequent debilitation of this freedom, so that it rarely poses a threat to orthodoxy (and never in some disciplines), could result in a situation in which it becomes little more than window-dressing.

If even the narrow conservative and liberal views of the purpose of a university demand more democracy in its governance, how much more is this true of the third, radical, view. In a context in which there was a two-way right of criticism and influence between the university and society, any monopolization of power authority or access to means of communication, would be absurd, as well as ineffective. The widely-felt need for change has therefore resulted in the devising of a wide variety of schemes for democratization, from on the one hand a kind of academic 'guided democracy' through to anarchistic academic communes on the other. The most carefully thought out and detailed of such schemes have been prepared as submissions to the review body at Birmingham University by the local branch of the Council for Academic Freedom and Democracy. Their proposals include the merging of all tertiary institutions in the Birmingham area to form a comprehensive 'polyversity', but most of the recommendations would apply also to single institutions. In what follows I have tried to summarise and reinterpret their ideas for the more general case.

Three main principles underlie the scheme for reform of the institution as a whole. Firstly, decision-making and management should be devolved to the lowest practicable level, in the interests of democracy and a participatory educational environment. There are few decisions that have to be made or implemented centrally. Secondly, decision-making at whatever level must be *open*, must provide as a matter of right, opportunities for full participation by the relevant section of the community, and must be conducted by people who are fully accountable to that community. Thirdly, the decision-making and management processes must be subject to frequent review, so as to promote appropriate development and flexibility.

The first step in the democratization process must be the reform of the smallest unit, the department (although, as a part of a wider democratic whole, other groupings would probably develop in this capacity). The three principles have two main consequences. First that the department should be recognized as consisting of every member – teaching and research staff, postgraduates and undergraduates, technical, secretarial and manual staff. Secondly, professorial headships should be abolished and the present functions shared among the members, particularly the academic staff. Departmental business should be conducted through a committee consisting of elected delegates of the various groups of members just listed. In particular, there should be substantial student membership (at least one third). There should be an elected departmental chairman, whose period of office would be limited, and general assemblies of the department to discuss major matters of policy should be held on a regular basis, with provision for an agreed number of members to call extraordinary meetings. The committee should not have any reserved business, except by common agreement, and the principle of delegates reporting back to their constituencies should be the norm.

Departments as they exist at present are very heterogeneous, in character and in size. They also, often more-or-less arbitrarily, separate disciplines which should be cooperating. They should therefore be grouped in schools (much smaller than present faculties in general), consisting of 500–1000 members, so that an average university would have about ten schools; polyversities would have many more. The major power of the community would be in these schools. They would make contracts with the university for a period of about six years, and, subject to co-ordination of their activities at a higher level, would be autonomous, with full power over resources, decision-making and administration. At the end of the six-year period, schools would review all courses, other teaching and research activities, and their inter-relations, before drawing up a new contract with the university.

Each member would have an equal say in the running of the school, with one vote. A committee of about twenty people should be elected for two or three years (perhaps one year for students), which would be responsible for the day-to-day running of the school. Its chairman should be freed of all other responsibilities for the period of his office. The committee would be responsible to a representative school board of around a hundred members (mainly concerned with medium-term matters), and the latter in turn to a general assembly of the school, meetings of which should be held regularly and, extraordinarily, on demand.

Court, council and senate as now constituted should be abolished, and replaced by a *court of representatives*, a *representative senate*, and a *general assembly of the university*. The first of these, representing society, should be of about fifty members only, including school teachers, parents, trade unionists, businessmen, etc., but it would have only advisory powers. The representative senate would be elected, with equal numbers of staff and students, and would become the titular and real sovereign head of the university. It would thus combine the powers and functions of both the present council and senate, as well as the formal legal authority at present nominally held by court.

The representative senate would be for the greater part of the time a coordinating body, ensuring communication between the schools. It would therefore include delegates from school committees, as well as delegates elected from wider constituencies or interest groupings. There would be a few centralized committees directly responsible to the representative senate, but these would be *functional* committees, concerned with works and maintenance, the library, the university centre, negotiation with outside bodies, etc.

All members of the university would belong to the general assembly, which could be called and attended by two or more schools. It would have the power of advice to those schools, and to the representative senate. Decisions of the latter (but not the former) could be referred back by it for further consideration.

These proposals mean that the government of the university would evolve in such a way as to combine direct democracy (at the level of the smallest units) with representative democracy (in the representative senate, etc.). The point about evolution is important: the groupings represented would at first be currently existing ones, but provision for review of the system should allow informal groupings to crystallize and gain recognition and representation.

The foregoing outline should have provided some of the principles on which the democratization of a university or polyversity could proceed. Several important issues have not been dealt with, however. The most important of these concerns the structure of the institution's relations with the wider community, in particular the method of financing it. In a more democratic community, the polyversity and other institutions – both productive, such as factories, and service, such as hospitals and schools – could relate to each other and a 'representative council' in a manner similar to the one indicated between the proposed schools of the polyversity. To what extent our present partial democracy would be prepared to finance more fundamental democracy in some of its institutions is in doubt.

The purpose of this article has been to show the connections between the functions that such an institution performs and its internal structure. If society is content with academic ivory towers that mind their own business, or alternatively prefers a trained-personnel production line, it will not take kindly to the 'subversion' and interference that would result from their democratization. A healthy democratic society would expect universities to be vital, annoying, influential, unpredictable, fallible, but indispensable, components of itself.

# Robert Benewick
## Universities: The Teaching Relationship

Robert Benewick was educated mainly in the United States and received his Ph.D. from Manchester University. In the early 1960s he taught in the West Indies; he has been lecturer in political studies in the University of Hull since 1963. He is co-editor of 'Readings on British Politics and Government' (1968) and the author of a study of British Fascism, 'Political Violence and Public Order' (1969) and editor of a symposium on violence in British politics, 'Direct Action and Democratic Politics' (1972).

Events of recent years have shown the persistence of a strongly anti-democratic tradition in the universities. Since knowledge is power there is a built-in elitism in any education system, for universities educate those likely to assume the command posts in society. This technocratic elitism is exacerbated by a lingering elitism associated with the traditional idea of the British university as educator of the ruling classes. The problems now facing us are, to some extent, the result of the democratic ethos, to which society is nominally pledged, breaking into the existing pattern of university education. Yet the commitment to equality of opportunity which underpins recent university expansion represents at best a half-way house to an egalitarian society in a culture where deference to authority is deeply rooted. In so far as the university situation and the teaching relationship foster elitist values and reflect and reinforce this deference to authority, neither an egalitarian society nor excellence can be achieved.

By excellence I mean more than the acquisition and systematic ordering of knowledge, for the purpose of the university extends beyond the education of intellectual astronauts. The teaching relationship must also enhance understanding and encourage creative thought. There are many features of British universities which actively contribute to the attainment of excellence. Where universities preserve and express the values of the enlightenment a creative climate is provided. Many aspects of university life are congenial to a favourable teaching relationship. Despite expansion most universities are still viable units. The staff–student ratio is much envied in other countries although little actual contact may occur. The examination system, despite its rigidity and despite the personal stresses it imposes, grants students a great deal of unstructured time as well as relief from day-to-day pressures. Students are offered a fair degree of flexibility of study within a fairly inflexible range of choices. Their personal lives are free from most restraints and the tyranny of conformity formerly associated with halls of residence is disappearing. Staff quickly achieve security of employment, pressure for publication is more indirect than direct and they enjoy a relatively high social status. The lecturer is free to teach without interference, although to a large extent without recognition.

Excellence in teaching, however, means a successful series of relationships, and there is much in the university situation to militate against this. At a time when universities are a centre of public debate it is ironic that they have themselves become less than before the arena for the free-play of conflicting ideas. This is not to deny the university its virtues. Nor is it a plea for its politicization. It is a comment on the growing incapacity of the university to provide a stimulating and challenging milieu for its students. The preoccupation with the preservation of cherished prerogatives relegates the student and the classroom to a secondary consideration.

Much attention has recently been paid to a supposedly new-style student whose commitment to the university is marginal. Less has been said about the way in which the university contributes to low student morale. The university is in a unique position, for at one and the same time it is involved in and detached from society. As a consequence of its involvement it tends to be a reflection of a society unable to solve many of its problems and simultaneously it abdicates its advantage of detachment as it ceases to be a testing ground for ideas. Its propensity to minimize controversy, moderate conflict and avoid intellectual debate is such an abdication. Symptomatic of this creeping intellectual paralysis is the reluctance on the part of the university teacher to submit his work to the criticism of his colleagues and his students for fear of losing his place in the queue for publication and promotion. Excellence is sacrificed to productivity. Curiosity is exchanged for careerism. Co-existence is substituted for involvement. Community is transformed into institution.

Both the older aristocratic tradition and the newer technocratic elitism of universities inhibit creative thought and constrict communication; as a result they ultimately detract from the attainment of excellence. Although a university, like most institutions, is organized in a series of authority relationships, it is not the imposition of its authority that matters so much as the deference which it expects and gains. The prestige of the university and its presence at the apex of the educational system ensures a high degree of compliance.

A minority of students may question the kind of society they are being prepared for, but for the majority the awards made available by expanding opportunity are too attractive. This induces a form of deference which tends to dominate the teaching relationship. The university teacher gains the student's respect because of his position rather than by what he teaches and how he teaches it. It is possible to teach American politics, for example, and only mention in passing the problem of a military–industrial complex, Black Power, poverty and urban violence. This must bewilder even the most bovine of students. Yet no one protests. At the end of an academic session I asked one of my classes what they would like to discuss at our final meeting. Only one suggestion was offered. Would I tell them what I really believed! Perhaps beliefs, opinions, speculation and the discussion of what some academics would dismiss as 'news' are more appropriate to informal occasions. The deferential atmosphere that surrounds even these occasions, however, tends to radiate paternalism rather than inspire intellectual exchange. As a result the teacher often turns away from teaching, at best with guilt and impotence, at worst with arrogance. He devotes his energies to research, if not to satisfy his creative urge, at least to advance his career.

The values of technocracy can also contribute to inequality

and to the discouragement of creative thought in the teaching relationship. The commitment to a discipline may supersede the commitment to the university, creating a situation where the teacher is unable or unwilling to communicate with his colleagues, let alone his students. The fashionable idea, the currently accepted approach, the esoteric language, the rigidly defined research project where the results can be quickly published, and the orthodox behaviour to impress those whose patronage is desired, are accepted by many as the stuff of professional standards. Insistence on quantification or highly specialized research, although not necessarily trivial, may mean that an interested and competent audience is unavailable. The professional conference is transformed from an intellectual to a social occasion. The departmental seminar, sometimes attended by students, is excellent in intention. Yet the subject matter is often too remote to encourage intelligent discussion. This compartmentalization sometimes spills over into the teaching relationship when the lecturer baulks at straying from his own narrow interests. Excellence is prone to be equated with disinterested research which may be nothing more than uncritical adherence to conventional professional standards or to the prevailing values of society. I sympathize with a student who wrote: 'There is something obscene in the way in which academics probe with their clinical fingers into the anatomy of revolution.'

Students are not immune from what passes as professionalism. One effect is the displacement of problems which students find relevant or necessary to university life. Another is the encouragement of the attitude that it is for the student to understand rather than for the teacher to communicate. One group of students spent their time in lectures preparing a content analysis of their teachers' material and produced a jargon-filled pastiche which they labelled the 'model social science lecture'. The general response seems to be that of mastering a number of techniques and suppressing critical faculties. An encounter with a former student elicited the remark that he had left university 'an educated hack'. He was quite pleased, however, for this is what his employers required. With further probing he admitted that university taught him to forget his own opinions.

The gap between the initiated and the uninitiated is aggravated by university structure. Observation must focus on the professorial role, for collectively the senior members of the university personify its ideal and ego. The professor is expected to participate in the government of the university at the point in his career when he has most to contribute to research and teaching. It is not just a matter of the anachronistic Wednesday afternoon in some universities where lectures and classes are cancelled to enable senior members to attend meetings and students to play games. The distinction between self-government and self-administration is not clear-cut, so that despite delegation to professional administrators within the university and to junior colleagues within the departments the professors' burden can be crushing. The price is not only expensive in personal terms but also in regard to the teaching relationship. Because of his status, his responsibilities and the demands made upon his time, the professor is remote from his staff and students. He is anxious to ensure consensus and conformity and to discourage restlessness, whether personal, political or pedagogic. The scarcity of senior posts which vests power, real and imagined, in the hands of a relatively small number inspires the junior staff and the students to caution. Intellectual life is further restrained.

I have tried to suggest that inegalitarian attitudes and arrangements endemic to the university situation are a deterrent to excellence. Liberals within the university, having derived satisfaction from apparent progress towards an egalitarian society, find themselves bewildered by student unrest and behave in ostrich-like fashion about the retreat of liberal values. There is much in the so-called cult of youth that is obnoxious, particularly its intolerance, commercialism, drug-culture language and anti-intellectualism. These are a reflection of, as well as a reaction to, prevailing values. This cult is also indicative of an undermining of deference and the need and confidence to communicate as equals. By countering the former values and furthering the latter, a meaningful teaching relationship can emerge in which student and teacher are equal in terms of the recognition of their respective worth. The university provides students with the opportunity to acquire knowledge and skills. It also provides time for reflection, but then so does a desert. How this time is used is dependent upon the teaching relationship. Intellectual participation and stimulation are necessarily nebulous concepts but unless they are included in the terms of reference, at least in the long run, university reforms may amount to no more than pacification.

## Postscript

I have deliberately chosen to let the preceding passages stand substantially unaltered for the second edition of this book. When they were written it was my firm conviction that the issues at stake in British universities were essentially liberal and furthermore parochial ones. Although some of the problems could not be divorced from the structural defects of British society, they were essentially marginal to it. Stripped of their rhetoric, student demands and university responses could be resolved within the realm of liberal discourse and liberal solutions. Indeed, contributors to the Black Papers were anxious to profess their liberal propensities. A period of quietude has descended upon British universities. This seems a mixed blessing, reinforcing those determined to preserve the *status quo*. The heady discussions of what a university is about and what the respective roles of student and teacher should be, have ceased and remain unresolved. I share with many the view that students seem to have lost interest in their work, or more appropriately, the work that university teachers conventionally set them. What I do not share is the view that the burden of blame should be placed solely on the student.

I have had no personal experience until recently of the British educational system outside the university. In December 1970 I was one of a number of university teachers who accompanied 700 British sixth-form students on a tour of the West Indies. What impressed me most was their interest, enthusiasm and willingness to learn, which stood in marked contrast to the students I normally teach, with the possible exception of the most politically radical. There was no compulsion, no examination and nothing to be gained beyond personal enrichment and understanding. This was more than a personal reaction, for I soon learned that every one of my colleagues was asking the same question: 'What happens to the student between school and university?'

There seems to have been a rise in student expectations which, despite token reforms, the universities are not satisfying. There has been little substantive change in the teaching relationship or in the subject matter taught. Relevance for its own sake, of course, is not what the teaching relationship is for. The job of the teacher is to show how problems can be studied, even where a system of cooperative selection of problems exists. Such a system, however, has yet to be sanctioned. With regard to subject matter, political scientists, for example, quick to adopt the more prestigious aspects of American political science, have tended to ignore the growing number of scholars who are looking at the political system from the bottom up rather than more traditionally from the top down.

The same criticism applies to the current approach to university reforms. We still look upon students as fortunate to be in university, soliciting their views, but setting the terms – then expressing surprise when views are not forthcoming. What we have learned is that it is difficult to achieve change. The need is for radical critiques and radical solutions.

# Raymond Williams
## The Teaching Relationship:
## Both Sides of the Wall*

Raymond Williams was an extra-mural staff-tutor in
literature at Oxford from 1946 to 1961, and is now
reader in drama and Fellow of Jesus College,
Cambridge. His publications include 'Culture and
Society' (1958), 'Border Country (1960), 'The Long
Revolution 1780-1950' (1961) and 'Communications'
(1962, revised 1968).

I was standing with a miner, a man of my own age, in the university museum at Oxford. The others had gone on ahead, past the
bones of the dinosaur, the neat glass cases of rocks.

'I can't explain to anybody what my work is,' he said suddenly. We had started that week talking about novels of working-
class life, in a summer-school literature group. The trip to the
museum was one of the regular afternoon excursions. Most adult
tutors know how, with working-class students, it isn't a question
of just teaching the formal hours. Until some other relationship
has been made, no teaching begins. Yet I still wasn't sure what he
meant. Was it a way of questioning the authenticity of the novels? We'd been discussing, that morning, why life in a working-
class home is so often described, the work itself hardly ever. So I
tried to bring what he said back to that. He went on looking past
me.

'I can't,' he said at last, with emphasis. 'Not them. Me.'

'You mean you've tried describing it?'

'Yes, talking.'

'And not got it through?'

'No.'

The museum was very quiet. He was watching me carefully.

*An earlier version of this article appeared in the *Guardian*, 26
September 1968.

'All right, try it,' I said.

He smiled, without sympathy, and then told me quite quickly. He was a roadmaker, underground. He had to follow and build the road to the face.

'Yes,' I said. 'I get the general picture.'

'Do you?' he said, with an aggressive edge.

'I think so, yes.'

'All right. Draw it.'

He took out a pencil and paper and handed them to me.

'I don't draw very well,' I began to explain.

'Try it,' he said.

I made a rough sketch and he watched me closely. It wasn't too bad, for he looked relieved, though he took the paper back and made a quick alteration of line. We waited some moments, and then went on to join the others. Some crucial point had been passed and the rest of the week went better. Yet I still go over and over this episode, as I try now to think, in very different circumstances, about the crisis in education, about communication and about the relations between education and democracy.

The first modern demand for what is now called student power came in adult education, for good historical reasons. It is an illuminating history, that long struggle by working men to get an education that answered their needs. Obviously they needed to be taught; they depended on men who through opportunity and training knew the things they wanted to know. At the same time, generation after generation, they insisted on sharing in the essential decisions: about what was to be studied, and how. Repeatedly, they set up their own institutions, and in this kind of self-organizing there was always a close relation between education and democracy – not simply the internal conditions, deciding what was to be done, but the external conditions, the relation between learning and what it was for, what the social process was for. The corresponding societies, the Hampden clubs, the secular Sunday schools, the cooperative circles, the mechanics' institutes, the Workers' Educational Associations, the labour colleges: we can learn more, now, from these, about the crisis in education, than from the more formal established institutions. For there was always a tension of a most complicated kind. Some people, always, wanted to control them (it was often easy through finance) so that what was taught was what the authorities decided.

But there was also authority of another kind: that which any teacher can feel, when a need for understanding is presented to him; that to get to D one must go through A, B and C; that, from his experience, the best way of learning is in this way and this – that, which you ask about, can only come later. But isn't it possible, the student replies, not always politely, that you're simply prejudiced; that you're not interested in D; that the world has changed since you learned your order of things; that anyway, if it hasn't, it looks different from where you are and where I am? At certain points of breakdown students have gone away on their own, distrusting established education and established teachers. 'Do you suffer from too much class consciousness?' the cover of *Plebs* asked ironically, at the time of a scheme for trade-union scholarships at Oxford. 'Try a term or two in the home of lost causes.'

I have been closely reminded of this history in the last year or two, in the new phase of the student movement and the free university. And there is some advantage in being able to see the problem from different sides of the wall. I had fifteen years as an adult tutor. I am now in my ninth year as a university teacher. In adult education the class meets, before the session, and decides the syllabus with its tutor. This was sometimes a formality, sometimes a combination of skilful persuasion and briefing, but often enough a genuine participation in the definition of educational ends and means. When I came back to Cambridge, as a lecturer, I found something of the same atmosphere; some optional papers and the need for selection within papers made a comparable process necessary. Again, I used to say, as an adult tutor, that I was in the only kind of education where students voted with their feet; if the class wasn't right, they didn't come. I had forgotten the Cambridge lecture system, in which attendance is optional and where, in English for example, only half the students ever attend at all. But this seems to me increasingly a negative freedom: the right to stay away (in fact often ignorantly or fashionably exercised) is no real substitute for cooperative decision. Teachers know too well the real errors, the glaring gaps, that follow from negative freedom. If some of them retreat into cynicism about students, which is now very widespread, they do not perhaps always realize that they, too, are victims of an inadequate system.

I have tried in my own teaching – lectures, classes and supervisions – to use methods I learned in adult education. But the difficulty of which everyone is aware is the examination system, which exerts its own, often separate disciplines. To have been free of that, in adult education, was of course an advantage, and it is not only because I hate examining (quite apart from not knowing what beta-plus-query-plus means) that I believe its radical reform is necessary. Yet it can only be changed responsibly if teaching is also changed, and these changes would demand more effort, more continuous and cooperative discipline than the present system. Students have above all to convince their teachers that they are ready for this. It is the problem of all social change: that a system produces kinds of human beings who then seem to illustrate the justification of the system. Breaking through to a different world involves not just the rejection of authority but the taking of authority, with all its consequent demands on oneself.

This new authority can come only from the difficult, prolonged and of course untidy process of cooperative decision. As a teacher, in adult education or at the university, I have often believed that I know what needs to be done, to understand a particular issue, and that this can involve unwelcome postponements, or tough and even boring preparatory work. But I have never known this refused, by a group, when it is fully explained. The challenge that the work can be done without it is, after all, easily met by detailed argument; or, if this is not so, if a proposed scheme can not be sustained, any teacher ought to know he must change.

In Cambridge this kind of discussion can readily take place inside a college, if the director of studies wants it. In several cases I know that it does. But in the last year we have been trying to get comparable procedures in the faculty as a whole. We argued for two terms about whether a joint staff–student committee or an open assembly was the better way; there were good reasons for both. In the end, for an experimental period, the Faculty Board created a joint staff–student committee (the students elected through colleges) to which it referred its general educational business. There are still serious problems of power: the Faculty Board can refer back the joint committee's recommendations and the university has to approve the decisions of the Faculty Board. All this is still a very active and contentious process, and of course may break down or move on into new forms.

But it is worth recording that the experience of the joint committee, and in particular of its working group on examinations, has seen, in my view, some of the most serious *educational* work of the year, just as some of the open meetings were among the best educational experiences I have known in Cambridge. So far from the caricature presented by the Right, in which 'concessions' are made to 'student demands' (and are of course always 'hasty, ill-considered and a betrayal of academic responsibility'), the process has seemed to me a beginning of the regeneration of the subject with a genuine widening of experiences and perspectives. In particular, a discussion of examinations reached the new principle teat examining is justified only in so far as it serves the learning rather than the assessment process, and that its methods need radical revision to that end. There was a surprising fertility of ideas designed to move responsibility for choice of course and method of study, in a developing way through the years, to the cooperative efforts of students and teachers, and away from the fixed syllabus.

This emphasis has now run into very heavy and very skilful opposition, and can be treated (at one level will have to be treated) as simple politics. But I want to record my belief, based on this experience, that the subject itself comes alive again, in new ways, as all its conventional procedures and assumptions are brought into open discussion. For of course these conventions (the decisions of our predecessors) are not the subject itself, or its only mode of seriousness. In all these detailed discussions, I have heard little proposed as a way of making the work easier (which is again the caricature drawn by the Right). On the contrary, what is mainly proposed is that the work should be more responsible and demanding, and that we should get rid of definitions and exercises which have a merely formal or habitual validity. I have felt more hope for my subject, and for its growth and continuation as a serious and lively experience, from this new cooperative discussion than from years of what are called the 'normal and appropriate decision-making procedures'. It is as a teacher, then, with that admitted and welcome responsibility, that I want to see this new work going on.

The real difficulty comes when this process is short-cut by external administrative decision, as happened all too often in the bureaucratic structure of some modern adult education, and as happens very often in universities, even when, as in Cambridge, the structure of the faculty is partly democratic (often, by that very fact, involving delays which can outlast any particular student generation). The toughest issue is not the complication of internal control, which with effort, patience and of course a necessary militancy of demand, can be got right. It is the very complicated question of social demand, and hence social control, of a public educational system. There have been some ugly attempts recently to exert repressive controls; and in any case the sophisticated financial management, by which control is really exerted in Britain, is now very dangerous to the universities, as it was constantly dangerous in the more exposed and poorer conditions of adult education.

I do not think these dangers have been at all sufficiently recognized. Indeed I sometimes feel that the whole public fuss about the student movement is a way of distracting attention from what can be seen as an attempt to reshape universities to the needs of a late capitalist and corporate society. And if staff and students can be set against each other (for which there are always plenty of local opportunities, real and contrived) this more serious threat will be overlooked or neglected. I happen to work in a faculty in which the staff–student ratio is 1:28 and in which admission to postgraduate work is effectively dependent on the grant decisions of the State. I find these limits and controls very much the most serious problem of my work as a teacher, and I believe that objectively (as well as in personal practice) I then have more in common with the needs of students than with any consenting, directing or authorizing establishment. This is a matter of simple daily experience rather than of any general belief. Yet a general understanding becomes necessary, if any real change is to come. And there I think it is very significant that just when higher education is of increasing importance in and to society, and the scale of investment correspondingly high, the old liberal attitudes of an earlier phase are not being extended to any wider democratic practice, but are being replaced, especially in new and untried institutions, but all the time more widely, by the techniques of appointed and co-opted authority (representing the power of the State and often of capitalist industry) and by detailed methods of financial and managerial control, using concepts quite alien to education.

I agree, in principle, that a society has a right to make demands on its educational system. I would like to see more public rows on this, not less, for I know I have to answer to, among others, the miner, on whose back an expensive system, directly benefiting now only a minority, must be seen to rest. It is in its way of meeting this issue that the most hopeful part of the student revolt can be seen. What students are often blamed for, inside the universities, is, to quote the caricature, 'asking us to meet them about the syllabus and then, instead, demonstrating about Vietnam'. The indefinite and unargued extension from the syllabus to Vietnam is of course irrational. But, in this real movement, the right questions seem to me to get asked: not only the local questions about research contracts with outside bodies, or about the giving of money for this, the refusal of money for that. But also, more generally, about who is speaking in the name of society; what real public decision is involved in the giving or withholding of public money; what version of society is implied in what are called educational requirements and standards. I think the student movement has been right to identify the present educational and administrative structure with the values of the bourgeois society which, in the nineteenth century, created it: the rigid selection and distribution of specialized minority roles, as against the idea of public education, in which the whole society is seen as a learning process, and in which, consequently, access is open, not only for all people but for all their questions, across the arbitrary divisions of quotas and subjects. This is what adult education embodied, as a demand, at once educational and social; in fact political. And there is good evidence to show that, in its genuine form, this extending education makes higher rather than lower demands, not only in intellectual quality (which a specialism or a minority can protect but not extend) but also, and crucially, in human recognition and response.

This is what I think I learned from my years in adult education, and that now helps me to see the true character of the university crisis. This is why I argue, in fact, not for student power but for democracy. What teachers have learned is also relevant, and will have to be part of any real reform. Much can be lost in the sillier rhetoric of generations, and the teacher who pretends he is not a teacher (of course also with much to learn) is a pathetic and irrelevant figure. But if there is discontent among students, there is also discontent among teachers, since we are all victims of the same system, and even those who play along with it usually have, in private, few illusions about what is really happening.

In these uneasy months, I remember the history of men without rights and without property demanding the means to understand and alter their world; the complicated interaction between their own self-organizing institutions and not only those who could control or buy them but also those who knew, from direct experience, how hard, disturbing and endlessly flexible any real learning is. I remember how many useless supposed short-cuts there are, in systems and in negations of systems. What I had to face with that miner in the university museum was the challenge to act as a man beyond a system of teaching, and yet to meet as we were, without either formality or pretence. It is what Tawney faced, in his adult classes in economics, on experience the discipline didn't yet include. And it is what a generation of adult tutors faced in the years since the war, on the real relations between culture and society, between democracy and education. These are the issues that at last, through a new generation, have reached the universities and that are going, not without difficulty, to change them.

# David Page
## Against Higher Education for Some

David Page read English at Oxford, took a Diploma in
Education and taught at the University of Marburg,
Germany. He spent some time painting in Greece and
St Ives, and then taught briefly at an Islington
secondary school, followed by seven years at Hornsey
College of Art during which time he helped edit 'The
Hornsey Affair' (1969). He became vice-chairman of
the Council for Academic Freedom and Democracy,
1970-71, and now teaches in the Department of Art and
Design, North East London Polytechnic.

It's not an accident that we talk about our education *system*; we
assume in saying it that the parts work together in the whole.
So they do, and because some of the parts are the wrong shape,
the whole thing works in a distorted way. Nursery education
for some, compulsory primary and secondary education for all,
followed by higher education for some again: we begin and end
with minority groups receiving privileged treatment. This has its
influence on what happens in the middle: it is the effect of higher
education on the structure below it which concerns me first.

For secondary schools higher education attracts and repels; it
is a magnet to the sixth former and a push in the face for the D-
stream, and the competitive tension it engenders within the
school ensures the devitalizing of the unsuccessful and the strait-
jacketing of the successful. Schools may try to concentrate on
the full development of the whole personality, but they can't
resist the pressures; it really isn't possible to opt out of a whole
State system. Even the fee-paying schools can't resist, since
they must ultimately compete for places in higher education like
everyone else.

The distortion shows in the concentration on hurdles –

GCE O-level, and then A-level. Inessential subjects – that is, those which don't assure university entrance – are pushed aside, and get a low quota of time and interest. It isn't just art and music (they've always been thought of as frills); now, it's even a bad idea to waste time on geography. This discrimination is reflected at University, where, strangely, the proportion of firsts among honours degrees in mathematics is about six times that for geography (Beryl MacAlhone, *Where*, March 1971). Within this narrowing of civilized concern there is also early specialization. Only by picking particular arts or science subjects at fourteen or fifteen can a child hope to be prepared in time. So there is a choice at a stage at which choice is absurd, because the alternatives aren't known. We say, in effect, 'You can choose either to learn how the total environment works, or what men have thought and done in it, but you can't learn both'.

While this sad charade goes on, the C- and D-streams have been created, all the way back into the junior schools. The kids say 'We know why we're in this class. We're the thickies, aren't we, sir? We're the puddens.' Like the lower orders in *Brave New World* they are conditioned to believe that they are dull, and that intellectual effort (which they identify with what the A-stream does, that is, the charade) is rarified, boring and probably enfeebling. Creative excitement, using one's brain at full stretch, is not an experience available to them, except through (say) football – where they believe it to be of a quite different order. If this sounds simply like the recounting of personal experience (which it is), I invite readers to look at an article by Rosenthal and Jacobson called 'Teacher expectations for the disadvantaged' (*Scientific American*, April 1968), which gives evidence suggesting that when teachers expect certain children to improve greatly, although the children have been picked at random, they do improve. An ominous finding here was that the children who gained intellectually when *not* expected to were looked upon as showing undesirable behaviour – were disliked by the teachers. (Highly creative, as opposed to highly intelligent, children also seem likely to clash with their teachers – see the essays by Getzels and Jackson and Wallach and Kogan in *Creativity* edited by P. E. Vernon, 1970. Discrimination against them continues up the system; consider the completely unjustifiable five 'O'-level

requirement for entry into Diploma in Art and Design courses.
Some LEAs are now (1971) refusing to give major awards to
students over eighteen on foundation courses leading to Dip.
A.D. unless they have two A-levels.) But then, isn't the conditioning necessary (says a small black voice), because, after all,
if everyone was educated, who would empty the dustbins?
Perhaps I exaggerate the cynicism, or even consciousness, of the
manipulators, but there is no doubt that the patterns of society
are acted out and reinforced in the structure of the school;
teachers take it as natural that a talented few should emerge to
take the few prizes – and the consolation is that it's hard luck,
that *everyone* can't win. (Why not?)

Those who rebel against all this tend to see the fault at their
own level, not as inherent in the articulation of the whole
system. They criticize their school, the examining boards, or
the universities, and propose reforms which can only be marginal.
Even those who try to look at the whole system can fail to identify what is going on. I remember, some years back, A. D. C.
Peterson trying to persuade the universities not to demand so
much sheer knowledge from entrance candidates so that early
specialization could be stemmed. In view of the forces involved
he had Canute's chance against the ocean, because GCE is
only a mechanism: it is there, precisely, to sift out of those who
want higher education a number equal to the number of places
there happen to be. Its standard has to rise by an inexorable law,
because the schoolchildren come to the examination better
prepared each year, and each school is obliged to raise its sights
to give its own children a sharper chance in the competition, and
so the vicious circle whirls on. The GCE examination takes
place because of some peculiar logic by which, if everyone has
competed according to the same rules, the result is fair. Of
course, it is a hopeless predictor of how people will perform in
higher education, and it takes no account of what they need;
fairness is hardly involved, since most of the competitors never
reach the start, and a lot of the rest carry handicaps (which
aren't however recognized by the rules).

The examination system – from the eleven-plus where it
hangs on, upwards – follows from the restriction of higher
education to an elite. So long as it is not available to all who want

it there will be some test or other to determine who may have it, and there will be a consequent distortion in the schools. Even 'equality of opportunity', that factitious Tory concept, cannot pretend to operate anywhere in the system while one sector of it is exclusive.

But is there in fact really a design (or conspiracy) to educate a convenient elite? Well, the Robbins Report (1963) says no:

> We have found the first approach [i.e. considering what supply of different kinds of educated persons will be required to meet the needs of the nation] impracticable. For, while it is possible, for a number of professions and over a short term, to calculate with a fair degree of precision what the national need for recruits will be, we have found no reliable basis for reckoning the totality of such needs over a long term.

Robbins therefore chooses 'considering what the demand for places in higher education is likely to be'. Now this suggests that they are *rejecting* a deterministic approach (hooray) – but only because it is too difficult (boo) – in favour of a humanistic one (hooray). But the implication that people, humans, you and I, are to be free to demand what we want is quite erroneous. The number of places needed is worked out by a tortuous projection based on the present population figures and assuming that the required minimum entrance standard will remain constant, along with the increase in those qualified (ch. 6). It's all jollied along by paragraphs like this one:

> In a system where almost all home students are assisted from public funds it is inevitable that there should be some degree of selection, and hence some degree of competition for entry. Moreover, we are anxious not to overstate the number of places needed. For these reasons our estimates do not allow for any relaxation of the degree of competition.

These people, I should explain, have all the basic requirements, so that the statement can only be justified by a mystical belief in the value of competition for its own sake. Anyhow, after all this, 'by 1980 this country should be providing entry to full-time higher education for about 17 per cent of the age group'. The Robbins team in fact side-stepped both possible approaches – they did not attempt to predict what is likely to happen in this particular advanced technological nation over the next decades (and those students of 1980 will be in mid-career in 2000), nor did they set up a model of a better society and aim towards it through education. As Robbins is not based on any vital analysis of society as it will be, or should be, ancient values filter into the vacuum: a faint skirl of 'Forward to Matthew Arnold'.

It isn't, after all, very difficult to forecast what is going to happen: change is going to happen, and far faster than ever before. For instance, the Swann Report (1968), (which followed the Dainton Report (1968) after the alarming news got out that the elite were choosing *not* to study science, and thus prospectively sabotaging society) shows evidence that the speed with which new ideas are translated into technical reality has been increasing: basic technology is changing so fast that there will have to be, in future, in-career re-education for technologists. But you can't have change happening in technology and not affecting society; life won't be confined to categories. It's also clear that change is deeply emotionally disturbing: the most distressing thing about the Hornsey and Guildford affairs is the way the squirearchy and the local authority would do absolutely anything to avoid the disturbance of what had to them become the natural order. What we must have is people who enjoy change (who don't just put up with it at a pinch). We need people who play with solutions creatively, like a child or an artist, and we need a society which does not, through built-in conservatism, prevent the putting into practice. The only way to prepare for such a society is to revolutionize education so that it teaches creative rather than defensive strategies. Our only choice, if I may heavily underline the point, is whether to ride the wave purposefully or flounder about in a life-belt: we can't stop the water. Also, since the problems of 2000 will be solved by the students of the 1980s, there isn't much time.

Higher education will have to expand far more than Robbins projected to cope with massive in-career re-education; this much will be forced by events, and in the short run it will be forced to expand fast (or else create an explosive situation), to accommodate the increasing number of qualified students. According to one estimate 'it does not seem outrageous to argue that there could be as many as 350,000 with five or more "O"-

levels, and 200,000 with two or more A-levels by 1980. These numbers represent increases of roughly 50 per cent and 100 per cent respectively on those used by Robbins' (see *Higher Education Review*, Spring 1970). But it is impossible to defend the present situation morally. As we approach our 17 per cent of the age group, at least 83 per cent are getting *no* full-time higher education. As Christopher Price, then a Member of Parliament, wrote (*New Statesman*, 7 February 1969): 'On Robbins's estimates, over a million qualified adults have missed out on this particular form of privileged education over the last three decades.' God knows how many it would be using estimates of ability and need rather than Robbins's 'qualifications'. And have these people now to spend the remaining thirty, forty or fifty years of their lives without that education? Robbins makes no provision for those who haven't made it up to now, nor for those who won't have made it in the next decades. It would be more honest, in the meantime, to stick pins in a list of those who want higher education, rather than to pretend that there is anything fair about GCE, with its verbal class-bias, its assumption that actual ability can be measured and potential ability predicted, and its dependence on the sweated labour of tired markers working to a deadline, who don't know the students or their problems and at best pride themselves on mechanical efficiency.

All this is usually justified by the statement that education is a rare commodity, simply not available for all. We can ask how many scientists are tied up in work officially labelled 'defence'; how many men are working on completely pointless commercial duplications and variations (see Keith Paton's provocative 'On Work and Surplus', *Anarchy*, December 1970). But argumentative skirmishing quickly gets bogged down in statistic and counter-statistic. The central point is that availability is not a fact, it is a decision. A rich society like ours, flowing with fridges and cars, can afford education for all. What I require here is that we should first make the moral decision, and only then explore the resources available for its implementation. Working the other way round always confirms the impossibility of doing anything but what we are doing.

The provision of higher education for all who want it also

implies *at any point in their lives*. At the moment there is a critical path to higher education, and if you don't get it by twenty-three or so, you might as well give up. Recently local authorities have refused to give grants to mature students who gained entry to further education colleges like Ruskin and Fircroft. The squirearchy and the local authority must economize on the odd ha'penny and who cares if the odd working man misses an education? In fact the mature student, who has been working, and who knows why he is back in education, would be voted by many teachers as the best student. The pressure on higher education from the eighteen-plus range is due to perfectly justified panic – it's now or never. Many students I have known have drifted out from college and become manual labourers or bums. I am sure that if they had first become manual labourers or bums, and had then entered higher education, they would not have found it so unrewarding (nor, come to that, allowed it to be so).

I don't regard 'Higher Education for All' as an ultimate aim. I hope we look forward to a society which will not draw a line between 'work' and 'education' – in which, indeed, 'work', 'life' (as its antithesis) and 'education' have become meaningless distinctions. But the interim need is for a fully educated society, which would be in itself radically different from ours. If we can't get this, we can kiss good-bye to dreams of participatory democracy, let alone the withering away of the State. Higher education for all who want it is the next necessary step along the way.

# References

**Abercrombie, M. L. J.** (1960), *The Anatomy of Judgment*, Hutchinson.

**Adams, P., Berg, L., Berger, N., Duane, M., Neill, A. S.,** and **Ollendorff, R.** (1971), *Children's Rights*, Elek.

**Anderson, H., Hipkin, J., Plaskow, M.** (1970), *Education for the Seventies: Transcriptions of the Cambridge Union Teach-In*, Heinemann.

**Banks, J. A.** (ed.) (1969), *Studies in British Society*, Routledge & Kegan Paul.

**Beard, R.** (1970), *Teaching and Learning in Higher Education*, Penguin.

**Benn, C.** (1970), *1971 Survey of Comprehensive Reorganization Plans and List of Comprehensive Schools, in England, Wales and Scotland*, Comprehensive Schools Committee.

**Benn, C.,** and **Simon, B.** (1970), *Half Way There: Report on the British Compr.hensive School Reforms*, McGraw-Hill.

**Berne, E.** (1964) *Games People Play*, Deutsch; Penguin, 1968.

**Birmingham University Staff Ad Hoc Group for University Reform** (1968), *No Easy Answers*.

**Boyson, R.** (1968), 'Threat to tradition', in N. Smart (ed.), *Crisis in the Classroom*, Hamlyn.

**Brosan, G., Carter, C., Layard, R., Venables, P.,** and **Williams, G.** (1971), *Patterns and Policies in Higher Education*, Penguin.

**Burgess, T.** (ed.) (1971), *Dear Lord James: A Critique of Teacher Education*, Penguin.

**Burt, C.** (1937), *The Backward Child*, University of London Press.

**Cammaerts, F. C. A.** (1966), 'The binary system in higher education', *Forum*, Spring.

**Carter, C. O.** (1970), *Human Heredity*, Penguin.

**Central Statistical Office** (1971), *Social Trends*, no. 2, HMSO.

**Chetcuti, F.** (1961), 'A study of the morale of A-stream and C-stream pupils in secondary schools with special reference to any differences in the attitude and behaviour of their teachers', *Educational Review*, November.

**Chomsky, N.** (1969), *American Power and the New Mandarins*, Penguin.

**Clark, H.** (1956), 'The effect of a candidate's age upon teachers' estimates and upon his chances of gaining a grammar-school place', *British Journal of Educational Psychology*, November.

**Cockburn, A.,** and **Blackburn, R.** (eds.) (1969), *Student Power: Problems, Diagnosis, Action*, Penguin.

**Cole, G. D. H.** (1952), 'Education and politics: a socialist view', *Year Book of Education 1952*, Evans.

**Collier, K. G.** (1968), *New Dimensions in Higher Education*, Longman.

**Council for Academic Freedom and Democracy, Birmingham Local Branch** (1971), First and Second Submissions to the Review Body at Birmingham University.

**Cox, C. B.,** and **Dyson, A. E.** (eds.) (1969). *Fight for Education: A Black Paper*, Critical Quarterly Society.

**Cox, C. B.,** and **Dyson, A. E.** (eds.) (1969), *Black Paper Two: Crisis in Education*, Critical Quarterly Society.

**Cox, C. B.,** and **Dyson, A. E.** (eds.) (1970), *Black Paper Three: Goodbye Mr Short*, Critical Quarterly Society.

**Crampin A.,** and **Armitage, P.** (1970), 'The pressure of numbers: speculation for the seventies', *Higher Education Review*, Spring.

**Crowther Report** (1959): *15 to 18: A Report of the Central Advisory Council for Education, (England)*, vol. 1, HMSO.

**Dainton Report** (1968), *Inquiry into the Flow of Candidates in Science and Technology into Higher Education*, HMSO.

**Daniels, J. C.** (1961), 'The effects of streaming in the primary school', Parts 1 and 2, *British Journal of Educational Psychology*, February and June.

**Department of Education and Science** (1965), Circular 10/65, *The Organization of Secondary Education*, HMSO.

**Department of Education and Science** (1967), Circular 11/67, *School Building Programme: School Building in Educational Priority Areas*, HMSO.

**Department of Education and Science** (1970), Circular 10/70, *The Organization of Secondary Education*, HMSO.

**Department of Education and Science** (1970), *Statistics of Education, 1969*, vols. 1–5, HMSO.

**Dobinson, C. H.** (ed.) (1951), *Education in a Changing World*, Oxford University Press.

**Douglas, J. W. B.** (1964), *The Home and the School*, MacGibbon & Kee.

**Douglas, J. W. B., Ross, J. M.**, and **Simpson, H. R.** (1968), *All Our Future*, Peter Davies; Panther, 1971.

**Eysenck, H. J.** (1971), *Race, Intelligence and Education*, Maurice Temple Smith.

**Ferri, E.** (1971), *Streaming: Two Years Later*, National Foundation for Educational Research.

**Ford, J.** (1969), *Social Class and the Comprehensive School*, Routledge & Kegan Paul.

**Gellner, E.** (1959), *Words and Things*, Gollancz; Penguin, 1968.

**Glennerster, H.**, and **Pryke, R.** (1964), *The Public Schools*, Fabian Society.

**Goodacre, E. J.** (1970), *School and Home*, National Foundation for Educational Research.

**Goodman, P.** (1971), *Compulsory Miseducation*, Penguin.

**Guilford, J. P.** (1967), *The Nature of Human Intelligence*, McGraw-Hill.

**Hadow Report** (1926), *Report of the Consultative Committee on the Education of the Adolescent*, HMSO.

**Halliday, M. A. K.** (1969), 'Relevant models of language', *Educational Review*, November.

**Hargreaves, D. H.** (1967), *Social Relations in a Secondary School*, Routledge & Kegan Paul.

**Hawkins, P. R.** (1969), 'Social class, the nominal group and reference', *Language and Speech*, April–June.

**Henniker-Heaton, C.** (1964), *Day Release, The Report of a Committee set up by the Minister of Education*, HMSO.

**Hirsch, J.** (1970), 'Heritability and racial intelligence, simplism and fallacy', *Cambridge Society for Social Responsibility in Science Bulletin*, special issue, July.

**Holt, J.** (1971), *The Underachieving School*, Penguin.

**Hornsey College of Art, Students and Staff** (1969), *The Hornsey Affair*, Penguin.

**Jackson, B.** (1964), *Streaming: An Education System in Miniature*, Routledge & Kegan Paul.

**James, C.** (1968), *Young Lives at Stake: A Reappraisal of Secondary Schools*, Collins.

**Jensen, A. R.** (1969), 'How much can we boost IQ and scholastic achievement?', *Harvard Educational Review*, Winter.

**Kee, A.** (1968), *Students at Hull*, Bertrand Russell Peace Foundation in Collaboration with the Democratic Education Group.

**Lewis, M. M.** (1963), *Language, Thought and Personality in Children*, Harrap.

**Lipset, S. M.** (1960), *Political Man*, Heinemann.

**Lunn, J. C. B.** (1970), *Streaming in the Primary School*, National Foundation for Educational Research.

**MacAlhone, B., and Rowe, A.** (eds.) (1968), 'Unstreaming in the comprehensive school', *Where ?*, Supplement 12.

**Macpherson, C. B.** (1970), 'The university as multiple fool', *Canadian Association of University Teachers Bulletin*, Autumn.

**Maclure, S.** (1970), *One Hundred Years of London Education, 1870–1970*, Allen Lane The Penguin Press.

**Mahon, D. F.** (1970), 'Language development in infants with reference to social deprivation', *English in Education*, Autumn.

**Marcuse, H.** (1964), *One-Dimensional Man*, Routledge & Kegan Paul.

**Marris, P.** (1964), *The Experience of Higher Education*, Routledge & Kegan Paul.

**Morris, W.** (1884), 'A factory as it might be', reprinted in W. Morris (ed.), *William Morris: Artist, Writer, Socialist*, vol. 2, Basil Blackwell, 1936.

**Morrison, A., and McIntyre, D.** (1971), *Schools and Socialization*, Penguin.

**Morrison, A.,** and **McIntyre, D.** (1969), *Teachers and Teaching,* Penguin.

**Newsom Report** (1963), *Half Our Future: A Report of the Central Advisory Council for Education (England),* HMSO.

**Norwood Report** (1943), *Curriculum and Examinations in Secondary Schools: Report of the Committee of the Secondary School Examination Council,* HMSO.

**Padfield, A.** (1969), 'The balance of frustrations', *Teacher,* 23 May.

**Pearce, R. A.** (1958), 'Streaming and a sociometric study', *Educational Review,* June.

**Pidgeon, D. A.** (1970), *Expectation of Pupil Performance,* National Foundation for Educational Research.

**Plowden Report** (1967), *Children and their Primary Schools: A Report of the Central Advisory Council for Education (England),* vols. 1 and 2, HMSO.

**Public Schools Commission** (1968), *First Report* and *Appendices,* HMSO.

**Reimer, E.** (1971), *School is Dead,* Penguin.

**Robbins Report** (1963), *Higher Education,* HMSO, Cmnd 2154.

**Rose, S. P. R.** (1970), 'The environmental determinants of brain function', *Cambridge Society for Social Responsibility in Science Bulletin,* special issue, July.

**Rosenthal, R.,** and **Jacobson, L. F.** (1968), *Pygmalion in the Classroom,* Holt, Rinehart & Winston.

**Rosenthal, R.,** and **Jacobson, L. F.** (1968), 'Teacher expectations for the disadvantaged', *Scientific American,* April.

**Rowe, A.** (1959), *The Education of the Average Child,* Harrap.

**Rowe, A.** (1971), *The School as a Guidance Community,* Pearson Press.

**Rubinstein, D.,** and **Simon, B.** (1969), *The Evolution of the Comprehensive School, 1926–1966,* Routledge & Kegan Paul.

**Russell, B.** (1916), *Principles of Social Reconstruction,* Allen & Unwin.

**Russell, B.** (1926), *On Education,* Allen & Unwin.

**Select Committee on Education and Science** (1969), *Student Relations,* vol. 1, HMSO.

**Simon, B.** (1971), *Intelligence, Psychology and Education: A Marxist Critique*, Lawrence & Wishart.

**Snow, G.** (1959), *The Public School in the New Age*, Bles.

**Spens Report** (1938), *Report of the Consultative Committee on Secondary Education with special reference to Grammar Schools and Technical High Schools*, HMSO.

**Stones, E., and Heslop, J. R.** (1968), 'The formation and extension of class concepts in primary-school children', *British Journal of Educational Psychology*, November.

**Stott, D. H.** (1966), 'Congential influences on the development of twins', *British Journal of Psychology*, November.

**Swann Report** (1968), *The Flow into Employment of Scientists, Engineers and Technologists*, HMSO, Cmnd 3760.

**Tawney, R. H.** (1931), *Equality*, Allen & Unwin.

**Taylor, W.** (1969), *Society and the Education of Teachers*, Faber. *Technical Education* (1956), HMSO, Cmd 9703.

**Thompson, D.** (1965), 'Towards an unstreamed comprehensive school', *Forum*, Summer.

**Vernon, P. E.** (ed. for British Psychological Society) (1957), *Secondary School Selection*, Methuen.

**Vernon, P. E.** (1968), 'What is potential ability?', *Bulletin of the British Psychological Society*, October.

**Vernon, P. E.** (1969), *Intelligence and Cultural Environment*, Methuen.

**Vernon, P. E.** (ed.) (1970), *Creativity*, Penguin.

**Wakeford, J.** (1969), *The Cloistered Elite*, Macmillan.

**Willig, C. J.** (1963), 'Social Implications of streaming in the junior school', *Educational Research*, February.

**Wiseman, S.** (ed.) (1967), *Intelligence and Ability*, Penguin.

**Yates, A.** (ed.) (1966), *Grouping in Education*, Wiley for UNESCO Institute for Education.

## Other Penguin Education Specials

### Death at an Early Age

*Jonathan Kozol*

The destruction of the hearts and minds of Negro children in the Boston public schools.

The discrimination that has made second-class citizens of one generation of coloured adults will as surely disinherit their children, future British citizens now in our classrooms, unless we urgently root out from ourselves – parents, neighbours, teachers, administrators – and from our teaching, our school books, our assumptions about language and thinking the subtle prejudices that, with a multitude of small cuts, wound the heart and mind.

*Death at an Early Age* is a moving personal testament from America: it also carries an urgent message for our society. Time for action may be passing faster than we think.

'Through Kozol's voice we hear the children calling for help. . . . I have heard enough Negro boys talking, not bitterly but jokingly . . . to feel sure that what Kozol tells us is the truth.'
*New York Review of Books*

## Letter to a Teacher

*The School of Barbiana*

Eight young Italian boys from the mountains outside Florence
wrote this passionate and eloquent book. It took them a year.
Simply and clearly, with some devastating statistical analysis of the
Italian education system, they set out to show the ways in which
attitudes towards class, behaviour, language and subject-matter
militate against the poor. They describe, too, the reforms they
propose, and the methods they use in their own school – the School
of Barbiana, started under the guidance of a parish priest and now run
entirely by the children.

This remarkable book was written for the parents of the Italian poor.
But it is about the poor everywhere: their anger is the anger of every
worker and peasant who sees middle-class children absorbed
effortlessly into the schools as teacher's favourites.

*Letter to a Teacher* was a best-seller in Italy and has been published
subsequently in many languages. The School of Barbiana was
awarded the prize of the Italian Physical Society, usually reserved
for promising physicists, for the statistical achievement involved
in the book.

'Hearing this passionate, angry cry from a few poor boys in a remote
Italian region, we dare not and must not dismiss it as an interesting
and exotic but irrelevant social happening in a country whose
problems are not ours. These boys *are* ours; their counterparts are
talking or shouting in school after school, on campus after campus,
the same message into our ears. We must learn soon, while we still
have time, to hear what they say.' *John Holt*

## Neill and Summerhill

*A pictorial study by John Walmsley*

A. S. Neill is the most famous schoolmaster in the world. What he has succeeded in doing at his school, Summerhill, has been perhaps the most important single reason for our increasing respect for school children as individuals.

This remarkable collection of photographs and reminiscences is a tribute to this man and his work. We once asked John Walmsley, the photographer, why it included so few pictures of Neill himself. 'The children,' he replied, 'are pictures of Neill.'

John Walmsley was born in 1947 and educated at Guildford School of Art. He has worked as a freelance photographer ever since leaving art school, and has had his work published in *The Times*, the *Listener*, *New Society* and *Camera*.

# School is Dead

*Everett Reimer*

Much of the sharpest and most fundamental thinking about education
has been coming from America. This book is one of five titles
published simultaneously by Penguin Education. It would be wrong
to call these writers a school – they are widely different in stance and
style. But they are united. firstly, by their readiness to think of
education in (literally) radical ways and to propose radical solutions;
secondly, by their deep concern that education should exist primarily
for the benefit of those who learn; and lastly, and above all, by their
conviction that education – in the modern world as in America – has
reached crisis point.

Most of the children in the world are not in school. Most of those
who are are drop out as soon as possible. Most countries in the world can
only afford to give their children the barest minimum of
education, while the costs of schooling are everywhere rising faster
than enrolments, and faster than national income. Schools are for
most people what the author calls 'institutional props for privilege',
and yet at the same time they are the major instruments of social
mobility. But at what cost in terms of true learning, true creativity,
true democracy? And at what ultimate cost to the societies which
perpetuate themselves in this way?

This is the background to Everett Reimer's important, wide-ranging
and intelligent book. The most urgent priority, he argues, is for a
consideration of *alternatives* in education – alternative content,
organization and finance. Above all, we urgently need alternative
views of education itself, its nature and possible functions in the
society of the future.